Paint the World with Love

Ordinary Adventists doing extraordinary things to change their corner of the world.

Jeannette Johnson

REVIEW AND HERALD® PUBLISHING ASSOCIATION
HAGERSTOWN, MD 21740

Copyright © 1991 Review and Herald® Publishing Association

The author assumes full responsibility for the accuracy of all facts
and quotations as cited in this book.

This book was
Edited by Raymond H. Woolsey
Designed by Bryan Gray
Cover art by Bryan Gray
Type set: Sabon 10/3

PRINTED IN U.S.A.

95 94 93 92 91   10 9 8 7 6 5 4 3 2

All Bible texts, unless otherwise credited, are from the King
James Version.
    Texts credited to NIV are from the *Holy Bible, New Interna-*
tional Version. Copyright © 1973, 1978, International Bible
Society. Used by permission of Zondervan Bible Publishers.
    Bible texts credited to RSV are from the Revised Standard
Version of the Bible, copyrighted 1946, 1952 © 1971, 1973.
    Verses marked TLB are taken from *The Living Bible,* copy-
right © 1971 by Tyndale House Publishers, Wheaton IL. Used by
permission.

R&H Cataloging Service
Johnson, Jeannette
    Paint the world with love.

    1. Christian life—Stories. I. Title.
        248

ISBN 0-8280-0631-8

Contents

Foreword

Putting this book together has been the fulfilling of a dream I didn't even realize I had. For as long as I can remember, whenever I'd see a crowd of God's saints, I would look into their faces and begin to wonder: Where had they been in their lifetime? What had they seen? What had they done? What was life like for them?

The truth is, most of us are rather "ordinary" people. We bloom and fade pretty close to where we sprouted. Most of the time that's in an out-of-the-way place where not many people pass by to admire our colors. Life would seem rather pointless if it weren't for one thing: the God who planted us not only has provided complete growing instructions; He knows exactly which "arrangement" needs our unique splash of color.

The best part is we don't have to worry about how to get into the bouquet. We just bloom where we are and leave the rest to God.

That's what this book is about—people doing the thing that lies in their path. Reaching out. Making a difference. It's a book of inspiration, encouraging God's dandelions to stretch toward the Son. Most of all, it's a book celebrating what God can do with a humble life given over completely to Him.

These are your stories. Ordinary people doing extraordinary things. Painting the world with love. But there are thousands and thousands of God's children whose stories are not recorded in this book. They are written in another, more important book, authored by One who sees every act of kindness.

"There is no limit to the usefulness of one who, by putting self aside, makes room for the working of the Holy Spirit upon his heart, and lives a life wholly consecrated to God. . . .

"God takes men as they are, and educates them for His service, if they will yield themselves to Him. . . .

"Men of the highest education in the arts and sciences have learned precious lessons from Christians in humble life who were designated by the world as unlearned. But these obscure disciples had obtained an education in the highest of all schools. They had sat at the feet of Him who spoke as 'never man spake' " (*The Desire of Ages,* pp. 250, 251).

A Special Word of Thanks!

We knew that every person has a special story to tell, but how were we to find those stories? As it turns out, all we had to do was ask! We placed ads in the nine union papers, asking for inspirational stories about ordinary Adventists who were making a difference in people's lives. And how you responded! You called us, wrote to us, sent tapes, letters, pictures, even a few family treasures. You told us wonderful stories about people you know and love. And in preparing your stories for this book, we've come to love them, too!

For introducing us to these new friends, we'd like to thank the following people:

Shirley Bolivar, Neil Busby, Ronald Busby, Ginger Church, Faith Crumbly, Brenda Dickerson, Bonnie Ensminger, Randall S. Fishell, Charles Gallimore, Kay Kuzma, Ruth Miles, Richard Orrison, Ron Peyton, Ron Quick, Deborah Reedy, Wendy Ringering, Karen Spruill, Carol Barron Thomas, Penny Estes Wheeler, and Rhoda Wills.

The Miracle of Giftedness

It's easy to look at a gifted musician, speaker, writer, or executive and say "I wish I had those talents. If only I had been born with that ability, then I'd work for the Lord!" But this reasoning is faulty.

I have discovered that giftedness is one of God's greatest miracles, lying dormant in His people until by faith they stretch themselves in service and, surprisingly, find themselves doing things they once would have thought impossible.

My life is a testimony to the fact that if God wants you to do something special for Him, He can give you everything you need, above and beyond your wildest imagination, in order to do that special work for Him.

When I stand before large crowds and speak without notes I hear comments such as "I wish I could do that." When others look at the book table filled with what I've written, they say "If only I could write like she does." At those times I want to shout "You can—if God wants you to do it!" It is my sincere belief that, if you are willing, you can do everything God wants you to do. You are gifted. Every one of God's children, regardless of handicap or life situation, is God-gifted!

I was a shy child. Secure in the stable home that Mom and

Kay Kuzma, Ph.D., is a noted child development specialist, parenting consultant, and speaker of the Family Matters *radio broadcast. She has taught for more than 20 years in the fields of child development and family health services at University of California at Los Angeles (UCLA), California State College at Northridge, and Loma Linda University and has designed and directed a variety of early childhood education and day-care programs.*

Kay is the author of more than a dozen books on the family, and serves as the editor and contributor for several periodicals on parenting and family living. She has been a guest on more than 100 local and national radio and television programs and is a popular speaker at conventions, church camp meetings, and women's retreats.

This is her story.

. . . .

Every one of God's

children, regardless of

handicap or life

situation, is God-gifted!

Dad provided for me, I knew I was loved supremely. Nothing in my early years can point to a reason for my feelings of inadequacy. Nevertheless, I was shy. From my first day in kindergarten when the teacher caught me talking when I was supposed to be resting on my little throw rug, I was afraid of failure and peer rejection.

In second grade I developed school phobia. Sometimes before leaving for school on spelling-test days I became so sick that I threw up. I remember turning around to my mom standing in the doorway and asking her once again how to spell a certain word.

In third grade I had a difficult time learning long division, but I was afraid to ask my teacher for help. I didn't want anyone to think I was stupid. We had the slow kids pegged—and that was one group I definitely didn't want to belong to. I had a cousin, Sharon, in the other third-grade class. They were slightly ahead of our class in the arithmetic book, so one day at recess time I waited in the girls' rest room until Sharon came in so I could ask her privately how to do the problems.

Fourth grade—oh, how I envied the five or six kids in our class who got A's in art. If only I could draw like they did. My work was definitely inferior—yet it was hung with the rest for the world to see!

Because of my shyness, I dreaded my fifth-grade reading class. We didn't have small groups. Instead, the teacher would make every child stand up and read a paragraph or two in front of the whole class. If one made a mistake, 30 kids would laugh! Most of the time the teacher would walk up one row and down the other, calling out a student's name when it was time to read. Once I had established her pattern, I would desperately try to count the paragraphs ahead and practice mine so I wouldn't make a mistake when it was my turn.

One awful moment is frozen in my memory. One day my teacher looked at me and nodded. I stood up to read—and my mind went blank. Though it happened 40 years ago, the humiliation of that experience still causes me to panic when I am asked to read something unfamiliar in public.

From seventh to tenth grade I attended a little church school in Boulder, Colorado. Because of my strong academic background from the progressive public school I had previously attended and my superior training in sports (especially in baseball), I came to this little school with some skills that were highly valued. I was immediately accepted into the most popular group—the only group. We had just five girls and one boy in our class! My confidence with this small group of friends carried me through my high school years at Campion Academy, but it shattered once again when I found myself separated from them in a Southern California college thousands of miles away.

I looked around the campus and saw Jaguars and Porsches in the student parking spaces. I went to classes and heard things being discussed that I didn't even know existed. I presumed the majority of students were rich and must have had IQ's of 200 or more! I was definitely not in their league. Once again, I began to pray that my professors wouldn't call on me, and I avoided social situations where I might not be accepted.

I even dreaded going to the cafeteria if I didn't have a friend with me. What if I had to sit by a stranger? Or worse yet, what if I'd have to sit alone? So I'd go through line and pick up a cup of yogurt and eat it in my room.

God knew what I needed if I was to do the work He had ordained for me to do. I needed someone who saw my potential and would encourage me to continue my education. So He brought Jan Kuzma into my life. Jan was the first person to encourage me to go to graduate school. It had never entered my mind. I felt lucky to get a college degree in what I perceived to be one of the easiest majors in college—home economics.

When I sent in my application to Michigan State University for a scholarship or teaching assistant position in general home economics, I had no grand and glorious idea of what I would do with a master's degree. I just wanted a husband. Jan looked good to me, but he was in the middle of a doctoral program at the University of Michigan. Obviously, if we were going to get better acquainted I'd have to move in his direction. The graduate degree at Michigan State was his idea. He pointed out that the two schools were 70 miles apart, a safe enough distance that my mom wouldn't get too panicked about our proximity to each other!

My application for financial assistance from MSU came back, stating there were no scholarships or assistantships available in general home economics. I would have to choose a specific area of concentration. I hadn't the foggiest idea of what I wanted to do with my life, but I read down the list: food and nutrition, clothing design, home management, interior decorating, child development . . .

I stopped at that point. "That's what I want to do some day," I said, "develop my own children." So I checked "child development." At that moment I knew nothing about the field or future job possibilities. Neither did I have any prior training that would qualify me for advanced study. But it was at this point that God worked the first of a series of miracles that completely changed my life.

I received a teaching assistantship in child development. A door that should have been closed swung wide open. I loved my courses. It was a revelation to me to realize that if I could figure out why children were doing the things they were doing, I could change the situation and significantly change their behavior.

After Jan and I were married, we carried our graduate degrees with us to UCLA. Jan was on the research faculty. I taught 3- to 6-year-olds in a multi-age, team-teaching, early childhood education unit of UCLA's University Elementary School, one of the most prestigious demonstration schools in the country. I now knew what I wanted to do in life—get my California teaching credential.

I was in an ideal situation to take some interesting education courses at UCLA and do some student teaching with older elementary children. After completing two years of teaching, which I knew would count for the remaining half of the state-required student teaching requirement, I sent in all my transcripts, knowing that I was almost over-qualified for a teaching credential. After all, I had not only a master's degree and an impressive number of graduate courses from UCLA, but I had proven myself to be an effective teacher.

I was shocked, therefore, when my application was denied. A door I had presumed to be wide open slammed in my face. They rejected my two years of teaching experience on a slight technicality: not all the children I was teaching were kindergarten age! I was angry at this seeming injustice and complained to Jan.

"Why don't you get your doctorate?" he replied.

A doctoral degree? Impossible! With my IQ I was lucky to get through college. Never in my wildest imagination had I ever considered a doctorate. But I was still a young bride, so I did what my husband suggested and talked to an advisor for UCLA's doctoral program in Early Childhood Education. After reviewing my transcripts, he told me I had already completed about half the course work—and I sailed through the program.

After my research was complete and bound in an impressive volume, ready for my dissertation committee members to ceremoniously sign, I received a form letter from the Records office. "Because of your low Graduate Record Exam scores, please make an appointment to discuss continuing your doctoral studies."

I couldn't believe it! In a few weeks I would be graduating with honors. When I explained this to the Records office they apologized for their mistake. But it wasn't a mistake. I had taken the GRE at a time when I had no interest at all in graduate school. I'm sure the scores were low.

Now, as I look back on the experience, I see that getting this letter at the end of my program was God's way of making sure I realized that my degree was not something I did by myself. It was His gift to me. If the Records office would have discovered my low scores at the time when they were considering my acceptance I would have been denied the possibility of proving myself. God must have known that I would need the knowledge and confidence of a doctoral degree in order to do the work He had for me to do.

What about writing? Certainly I must have had natural abilities in that area. No! I have learned to write by writing.

> **A door I had presumed to be wide open slammed in my face.**

15

It was the first New Year's Day after our marriage. Jan and I were making New Year's resolutions. "Honey," he said, "God has given us our educations [he had his doctorate; I had a master's]. We really ought to share some of the special knowledge that He's given us with others who haven't been so privileged. Let's each write an article for the church paper this year."

I laughed. I knew I wasn't a writer. He wrote two articles. Both were published. I began to feel guilty that I had let my new husband down, so I wrote a three-page, double-spaced article and sent it off, certain it would be published. I received a page-and-a-half, single-spaced rejection letter with detailed recommendations for changes that would need to be made before my article could be published. That did it! My writing career was over.

A number of years later, I read an article in that same church paper on spanking—how long, how hard, and with what instrument. I was angry and yelled at Jan, "Why didn't they tell the importance of parent-imposed, logical consequences and behavior modification? What about considering the reasons why children misbehave instead of just spanking them?"

"Don't yell at me," Jan said. "If you feel so strongly about it, write an article in rebuttal."

I did. I was so upset I poured out my soul, and in three hours wrote a masterpiece. I gave the article to Jan, and he edited it for six weeks before we submitted it for publication. When I saw that article in print, something happened to me. It was as if the Lord had put a burden on me to write. Every night after the children were tucked in, I sat down at my typewriter and wrote until about 11:00.

Before long, other articles were published, then books began to appear. Jan finally got tired of editing my work and suggested that I take a creative writing course. God prepared a dedicated Christian writer to inspire and mold my writing skills into what they are today.

What happened to my shyness? I'm still shy—unless I'm doing what I believe God wants me to do. For years, because of my feelings of inadequacy, I made speeches using copious notes. That

I'm still shy—unless

I'm doing what I believe

God wants me to do.

16

changed the day I was to give the sermon at the Garden Grove Seventh-day Adventist Church. We arrived early, and 20 minutes before the morning's program was to begin I was asked if I would speak for Sabbath school, too.

I had nothing prepared. There was time only to jot down five words (an acronym that would later form the basis for my book *Filling Your Love Cup*):

C = Care
R = Respect
A = Acceptance
F = Forgiveness
T = Trust

I quickly thought of one story to illustrate each of these five characteristics of love, and then I fervently prayed that God would fill in the rest.

A few minutes later, I spoke without notes for the first time in my life. Afterward, I walked off the platform, exhilarated over what God had done. It was good. I had totally enjoyed it—but it hadn't been me!

Based on that experience, I decided that God was much better at speaking than I was, and except for rare occasions I have never again used notes. I prepare a mental outline of three to five points and then rely totally on what God inspires me to say.

Can you see why I believe giftedness is a miracle? Today, when I'm sharing what God has given me, I can get up in front of the largest crowd or the most impressive television camera crew and not be afraid. However, if I'm in a small group of strangers and someone suggests that we introduce ourselves, I panic. I feel fear in the pit of my stomach as my turn to speak comes closer—the same kind of panic I experienced in that fifth-grade classroom almost 40 years ago when I stood up to read!

I'm still shy. But with God I don't have to let it control me. When I'm doing God's work I have no fear! Instead, I'm free to use the gifts that He has given me to use. It's a miracle!

You too are gifted. I encourage you to stretch yourself in His service and experience the exhilaration of giftedness you never thought possible.

"Without God, it is utterly impossible. But with God everything is possible" (Mark 10:27, TLB).

It's true. I've experienced it.

Miss Clown

Angels come in many guises. Her guise is as a clown. And although not many people outside her circle of family and friends know her name, she's probably one of the best-known people in several counties.

It all started five years ago when Madeline Rains was longing for a way to share her love for Jesus with the people in her small Tennessee home town. One day she decided she'd just go the length of the main street and give out copies of *Happiness Digest, Great Controversy,* and magazines and papers she had collected from church. To her dismay, nobody seemed to want what she was offering.

"You know how it is." Madeline laughs gently, the sound of the Tennessee hills singing in her voice. "Sometimes when folks have a little money, their noses tip a bit high in the air when they get around us poor folks!"

She didn't think of giving up for a minute. She was sure of her mission. She would just have to work out a different strategy. And she did the day the parade came to town.

It was the usual kind of parade—marching band, waving flags, clowns darting here and there, making people laugh. How people enjoyed the clowns! Everyone wanted to talk to them. Even the "snooty" people, Madeline noticed.

So she went home and made herself a clown suit, complete with orange wig, red plastic nose, and oversize feet.

She talked her daughter into driving her down town that first time. The girl parked the car in an alley and turned to her mother. "Mama, I love you very much," she said, "but when you get out of this car, I want you to know you're on your own!"

It turned out just as Madeline had hoped. "Everybody talks to a clown," she says. And they were happy to accept her books and

19

papers—the doctor, the pharmacist, all of them. One thing led to another, and word got around that "Miss Clown" also collected clothing to share with the people who lived in the housing projects and up in the hills. She had no place to keep all the clothing that was donated except in her guest room and her car.

"I just hope that trunk lid never springs open and scatters clothes clear to the next town," she laughs.

On the days the commodity people come to the housing project to distribute surplus food, Madeline arrives at 5:30 in the morning, dressed in her clown suit and well supplied with balloons, to set up her table nearby. She carefully arranges the clothing, putting a paper or tract in each pocket.

When the people start coming at 8:00, she's ready. Once a crowd of children have gathered, she begins to read them a story from *The Primary Treasure* or *Guide*. Just when the story gets most exciting she suddenly gets "very busy" with customers and tells the kids they'll have to ask their mothers to finish reading the story to them!

Winters are cold around Kingston, and warm coats are scarce. So every fall Madeline has a coat give-away. She'll never forget the little girl who stood in line one year. "She must have been about 8," Madeline remembers, "thin and wistful." Everything about her shouted that there had never been enough of anything. When it was finally her turn, Madeline helped her slip into a warm woolen coat. The child began jumping up and down, shouting, "Oh, Mama, I have a coat for this winter!"

Madeline's ministry was growing. After the newspaper did a write-up about her work, people began to call, offering donations of clothing—and requesting help. A Baptist pastor, who ministered to a community of very poor people on Oak Dale Mountain, asked if she could find clothing for about 40 boys. (Boys' clothing is hard to come by—they usually wear their clothes out before they outgrow them.) Madeline called on the Community Services organization of the nearby Athens Seventh-day Adventist Church, who gave her 700 pieces of boys' clothing.

Just before Christmas in 1988 an 87-year-old woman who

> **Everything about her shouted that there had never been enough of anything.**

had read the write-up and seen Miss Clown's picture began asking around town, "Do you know Miss Clown?" She needed a coat. Badly. Finally, someone suggested that she call the newspaper. The editor knew immediately whom she was talking about and put Madeline in touch with her.

When Madeline drove to her little house in a neighboring town, it was filled with children, grandchildren, and neighbors, all anxious to see Grandma's new coat. Madeline had brought her two. The little woman didn't know which one to try on first, but finally selected one and buttoned it firmly under her chin. When Madeline left her, she was sitting in her rocking chair, regal as a queen holding court. She died 12 days later. It was good to have given such happiness.

Yes, angels come in many guises. Sometimes they stand in a cloud of balloons, reading to small children in a housing project. Sometimes they look like Mrs. Santa, bustling about rekindling the joys of Christmas in the hearts of old people shut away in a retirement home. Sometimes they look just like a caring friend, quietly working in the kitchen of someone who's lost a loved one. And for the hurting hearts, writing a special poem about the loved one and clipping it to a copy of *Steps to Christ* .

And sometimes, an angel looks like a clown.

Dinner for 50

Carol and Chuck Keith have a large family. In fact, their family is so big that in order to keep everybody up to speed with what's going on, they have their own newsletter that goes to a mailing list of 120. Most of their kids are in college. (And you thought you had tuition bills!)

Actually, the support they give their kids is not so much financial, although that's certainly part of it. Their support is of the most important kind: Carol and Chuck are always there for them.

"We didn't really plan on this; it just sort of evolved," Carol says with a delighted laugh.

In the early 1980s the Green Lake church in Seattle, Washington, got a new young adult chaplain and his wife, Michael and Gwen Brownfield. They enthusiastically began developing a ministry especially for young people who were attending the various universities and colleges in the Seattle area. They conducted Sabbath school classes, nutrition classes, Revelation Seminars, and vegetarian cooking schools. They organized a wellness club that encouraged the growth of the whole person—mental, physical, and spiritual.

They printed a paper, *Adventist Christian Fellowship*, listing not only the names, addresses, and phone numbers of Seattle area churches and pastors, but provided information about special programs and events. They printed up special informational brochures that were placed on the bulletin boards of all the local campuses.

Right about here is where Chuck and Carol came in. Pastor and Mrs. Brownfield lived 12 miles from the church, but the Keiths live only three miles away. And since the city buses conveniently run right by their house, the Keiths began sharing their Sabbath dinner with any university young people who showed up for church.

Then when the Brownfields were transferred to another church, the Keiths just kept fixing dinner. Eventually, dinner at the Keiths' came to be a standing invitation, not only for college students but also for any young adults or visitors who came to the Green Lake church on Sabbath. If Carol didn't invite them, one of the students would.

"It's a stressful society out there," Carol explains. "Many of these young people are living in the big city for the first time, attending a university where most people are not Adventists, or even Christians. Maybe they're starting their first job. They need a group of fellow believers they can gather with on Sabbath for Christian fellowship."

How many come to dinner each week? Anywhere from 30 to 45. No one is asked to bring any food—just to come. Carol does all the buying and cooking.

"They're so busy with school or their first job, they don't have time to cook," she says with perfect logic. "We have a simple menu and serve the same thing every week: apple juice, tossed green salad, frozen corn, and rolls. So the only new thing I have to come up with is an entree and dessert."

Even food shared with wonderful young people costs money, though. Who pays for all this? (I had to ask!)

Carol laughs. "Oh, the Lord sends us things in such wonderful ways, I wouldn't want to pass up His being able to do that! One Sabbath we had 39 guests," she continues, "and I didn't have enough dessert. Carrie, one of our girls, brought along two pies and two cakes. Another time there were 50 of us. The visiting parents of one of our kids brought two casseroles over. The Lord provides."

When the Keiths started this ministry almost 10 years ago, it was just Sabbath dinner. Then they began doing other things—a hike, a trip to the zoo or park, an occasional social in the evening.

Now they have a full-blown program. Once a year they hold a meeting. They decide who of their group is going to teach the

Sabbath school lessons in their young adult class during the coming year. (They teach in pairs, the same pair teaching the same week of each month, thus involving eight young people.)

The third Saturday night of the month is reserved for a social of some type, planned by the young people. They've enjoyed game night, video night, a progressive dinner, a Halloween party. They've had a chocolate desserts night and a Valentine party (Italian style). They've "been to France in the 40s" and conducted an annual pitch-and-putt golf tournament.

Three events have become yearly traditions. On a Sabbath afternoon in April they go to the second largest tulip-growing area outside of Holland. Dubbed their "Tiptoe Through the Tulips" event, they drive to Arlington, about 40 miles away, where they enjoy a picnic dinner and the beautiful park by the river. After lunch, they caravan through the nearby tulip fields, ending the day around a campfire singing songs and playing games.

In August everybody meets at the Keiths for breakfast. Then they carpool to Birch Bay, near the Canadian border, and spend the day on the beach walking, playing volleyball, and riding go-carts.

In September they take the ferry to an old army fort on the Olympia peninsula for a special weekend retreat at Ft. Flagler State Park. This outing can be summed up in three words—food, fellowship, and fun.

Over the years something happened to this group of strangers who began meeting for dinner on Sabbath. They began helping each other, whether it was moving to a new apartment or finding a compatible roommate. One of the young men lost his job and was very down on his luck. At Christmas time, several of the others got together and bought him badly-needed clothes and mailed them to him anonymously.

They didn't feel so charitably toward Matt (not his real name). He'd been coming to their group for some time, and there was a little problem. He seemed to be very tight with his money, always waiting for the others to pay for things. One day as everybody was sitting around talking, it came out that his parents

Over the years something happened to this group of strangers who began meeting for dinner on Sabbath.

24

had divorced when he was very young. Money was so tight that frequently they didn't have enough food. He used to go to friends' homes after school and stay and stay, hoping they would ask him to eat with them. That small insight into Matt's growing-up years changed the way he was viewed by the group. They were able to love him for who he was.

The young people are not strangers anymore. They're family, to each other and to the Keiths. "Nobody leaves our house without a hug," Carol says. "When they graduate and move away it leaves a hole in our hearts."

Mail from Japan, Switzerland, France, Chicago, Washington, D.C., and California finds its way back to Seattle. It's from people who received more from the Keiths than Sabbath dinner.

The Boy From Paducah

It wasn't that Claudie had anything against religion. It was just that in all his 20 years he'd had absolutely no exposure to it. So he really didn't have any feelings one way or the other that day he found himself standing across the street from the sports arena. Looked like something was going on over there. Maybe another wrestling match. He enjoyed those. Might as well go see.

What was going on over there was the last week of an evangelistic series. What he saw aroused enough interest that he decided to come back. And when the meetings transferred from the sports arena to the Seventh-day Adventist church a couple nights later, Claudie followed.

One night it was announced there would be a baptism the very next Sabbath. Might be interesting to find out what that was. When Claudie arrived, the person passing out white robes handed him one. Whoa, a minute! Last time he checked, he was still only in the curiosity mode.

He bolted down the center aisle and through the door. He had covered most of the church yard when he heard pounding footsteps behind him and felt a strong hand grip his arm. It was the evangelist, puffing but determined.

Claudie is a little vague on the particulars of the next hour or so, but he does know that the preacher somehow got him back inside the church and into a robe. Baptized him first, too. Probably a wise move, in light of what had just happened.

When Claudie came up out of the water, he now knew two things about religion. Somehow, during those five or six evangelistic meetings he'd attended, a single-minded flame of resolve that was never to be extinguished had been kindled in the deepest core of his being. No matter what, he was going to be faithful to God.

At this point, he had no clear idea how to do it; he only knew he would.

The second thing he knew about religion was that from now on he would be going to church on Saturday while everybody else he knew went to church on Sunday.

A few months later, he was drafted into the Army and sent to Ft. Knox for basic training. He left behind a girl he intended to marry. It was important to him that she become an Adventist first. So before he left, Claudie asked his pastor to give her Bible studies. Then he made her promise that she'd write to him in Korea and explain everything she was studying. That way, this boy who didn't even own a Bible could learn, too.

The first Sabbath morning his company fell out for formation, Claudie "disqualified" himself from the Army till sundown. There was no Adventist church on the base, nor, so far as he knew, any other Adventists. But he had noticed several other churches. So he made his way from one to the other until he found one whose door was open. Slipping inside, he picked up a red Gideon Bible from the rack and sat down in a pew. There, this guileless child of God from Kentucky spent the entire day all alone, reading and singing.

This became his pattern for the four months he was in basic training. If one church door was locked, he kept going from church to church until he found one that was open.

Of course, his absence during Saturday morning fallout was noticed and reported, and two officers eventually came to his barracks to question him. When he saw them coming, he got so scared he "didn't hardly have good sense." So he ran down to the basement of the barracks and hid behind the furnace.

It wasn't that he was afraid of what they would do to him. By the same "knowing" that he would be true to God, he knew God would fight his battles for him. No, that wasn't what was worrying Claudie. What he needed was help answering the questions those officers were sure to ask. That's what he was discussing with the Lord behind the furnace.

When he finished praying, he leaned out just far enough so the

This guileless child of God from Kentucky spent the entire day all alone, reading and singing.

27

light could shine on his Gideon Bible. It fell open to Matthew 10:28: "And fear not them which kill the body, but are not able to kill the soul: but rather fear him which is able to destroy both soul and body in hell."

As he read these words it was as though an electric current passed through his body. Stepping out from behind the furnace, he walked confidently upstairs to meet the officers. They questioned him for 20 minutes and left the barracks. And that's the last he heard of it, even though his sergeant kept turning in complaints.

Just as Sabbath belonged to the Lord, every other day belonged to the U.S. Army. Claudie kept everything inspection-ready at all times. His boots were always shined. His locker was in order, and a quarter thrown on his well-made bunk jumped a yard. He never failed to clean his gun as soon as he fired it.

Claudie always got good points at every inspection. Good points meant special privileges, such as going to the PX every night, and home every weekend that he could afford to. And going to the PX meant working on a way whereby he could afford to go home. Each night he'd buy seven boxes of candy and several cartons of cigarettes to sell the next day to his barracks mates who had failed inspection. By buying for four cents and selling for ten, he made a whole lot more than the government was paying him.

He'd been selling cigarettes for a month or so when his conscience got to bothering him. He couldn't account for it. He was just impressed not to sell them anymore, so he quit.

After basic training, his company shipped out for Korea, stopping over in Japan. Claudie's feet had scarcely touched land when he was in trouble for refusing a direct order. It was Sabbath, and he had to refuse to mop the kitchen floor. So he was hauled off to headquarters to await questioning.

"I won't know how to answer any of the questions they're going to ask me," he confided in another soldier waiting nearby.

"When they take us in," his new friend counseled, "just listen to what I say and you'll know what to do."

Unfortunately, his friend was moved to another section of the jail, leaving Claudie on his own. Two guards came to escort him

Just as Sabbath belonged to the Lord, every other day belonged to the U.S. Army.

to a cell. Sandwiched between them, Claudie proceeded down the hall. But before they reached the cell, the guards received word that they were to take Claudie by the colonel's office. Before the worried soldier had time to gather his thoughts, a door was opened and he was thrust inside.

There sat the colonel! Poor Claudie was so unnerved he didn't even salute, let alone give his name, rank, and serial number.

"Have a seat," the colonel invited.

Sitting on his bunk later, Claudie tried to remember their conversation, but his mind was blank. The Lord had supplied all the answers. The colonel had dismissed him by saying, "Private English, go back to your bunk. If anybody else bothers you, let me know."

Claudie's first contact with another Adventist soldier came during this layover in Japan. As an infantryman, Claudie had been trained not only to shoot every weapon the Army used, but had also become a sharpshooter. One day a Jehovah's Witness boy he knew asked him what faith he was. Hearing he was a Seventh-day Adventist, he said, "There's another Adventist soldier in our barracks. Want to meet him? I'll go find him."

True to his word, the Jehovah's Witness was back in a few minutes and introduced the two soldiers. While they visited, the other Adventist kept eyeing Claudie's gun.

Finally he blurted, "What are you doing with that gun? Seventh-day Adventists don't carry weapons."

Well, that's the first Claudie had ever heard of that! "How do I get rid of it?" he wanted to know.

"Go over to the officers' quarters, lay the weapon on the counter, and say you won't carry it anymore, that you're giving it up. Then walk away," the Adventist soldier instructed.

So that's what Claudie did. There was all kinds of trouble. The Army insisted that that was what he had been trained for and he would have to do it. They forced him to take the gun back, stating he would have to stay with it.

Knowing he shouldn't carry a weapon bothered Claudie so

> **Claudie had been trained not only to shoot every weapon the Army used, but had also become a sharpshooter.**

much he couldn't get any peace. Back he went to the officers' quarters.

"You know where you're going, don't you?" the officer shouted. "You're going right up on the front lines! If you want to go up there without a weapon, that's your business."

He was transferred over to tanks. But tanks have to be fired, too. Every day he tried to get help for his situation, but without success. There was no Adventist chaplain, so he sought out the Baptists, the Presbyterians, anyone who might help. By this time, the officers were making it so hard on him he was getting desperate. As a last resort, he decided to visit the Catholic priest.

Overnight Claudie was made a medic and sent to the front lines, not knowing how to do anything beyond putting on a Band-aid. But he learned it quickly, firsthand, as soon as he arrived in Korea.

He told his new officers right away that he would need to be relieved on Fridays about two hours before sundown. They laughed at him as though he was the craziest person they'd ever heard talk, and walked away. Nevertheless, when no replacement showed up that first Friday evening, Claudie walked off the front line.

That's not a healthy thing to do. Soldiers who walk away from the front line can be subject to court martial or even be put before the firing squad.

Once again Claudie asked the Lord to fight his battle for him because he didn't know how. He waited. Nothing happened. Nobody said anything, nobody did anything, for seven weeks. The seventh week they sent a replacement, and for the nine months Claudie served on the front line, a replacement came every Friday two hours before sundown.

It was strange, but the men in his company never harassed Claudie. There was something about him, a childlike transparency, that drew them, made them feel safe in that hellish place. When he knelt down to pray at night, the barracks went dead quiet until he finished.

Before men are sent to the front everything is taken away

When no replacement showed up that first Friday evening, Claudie walked off the front line.

30

from them—even their watches and calendars. All they have is their clothes, weapons, and dog tags. While the other men devised methods of keeping track of time, Claudie never did. He knew the Lord would let him know when it was Sabbath. On Friday afternoon, men would stick their heads out of their foxholes and call "Another week's past; here comes Doc!"

Claudie would meet with 35 or 40 other Adventist soldiers for Sabbath services in what was called the two-point zone, 15 miles behind the front lines. After their Sabbath service, they'd eat lunch, then break up into small groups to talk.

One Sabbath Claudie and another soldier, Carlton Freeman, walked three or four miles until they came to a creek. Carlton began telling Claudie what he believed about hell.

"I don't see it that way," Claudie said. "I've always heard that people in hell will burn forever and ever and ever."

Carlton didn't say another word. He just reached into his pocket and pulled out a big piece of paper and some matches. Wadding up the paper, he set it on fire. Both men watched silently until the paper was nothing more than a wisp of smoke.

"Now, Brother English, that's the way hell is going to be," Carlton said. "Hell's going to burn till it burns itself out, then that's the end. Like smoke arising from paper."

That's how Claudie began learning about Bible doctrines.

One Sabbath he went through chow line behind another Adventist soldier. As they began to eat, the soldier said, "That's pork you're eating."

"I know," Claudie answered between bites.

"Seventh-day Adventists don't eat pork."

Claudie stopped in mid chew.

His friend took out his Bible and gave him an on-the-spot Bible study on unclean meats. When he got back to the front lines, word filtered down to the cook that Claudie wasn't eating pork anymore. But when he even passed up the eggs one morning, the cook asked why.

"Because you fry them in hog grease," Claudie told him.

"Well, if I fix them in butter will you eat them?"

So he fixed the eggs in butter. He even worked out a way of letting Claudie know when anything had lard in it. "As you're going through line, if anything is cooked with lard, we'll shake our heads no," the cook told him. "But if it's OK, we'll shake our heads yes."

When it got to be just about dark on the battlefield, the men would begin looking for a bunker in which to spend the night. Often, Claudie would crawl into the nearest one of these holes in the ground and fall asleep. The other men would keep hunting until they found him. Sometimes when he woke up, 15 or 20 men would be in there with him. You were safe if you were with Claudie.

Often Claudie's crank radio would ring in the night, summoning him into no-man's-land to pick up wounded. Nobody wanted to go to no-man's-land. If a man didn't let his people know he was going out, he could likely get shot at, not only by the enemy but by his own troops. No, it wasn't a place a man went voluntarily. But when Claudie swung onto the jeep to make his run, he'd look back to see men hanging off every available inch of the vehicle. It was safer in no-man's-land with Claudie than in the foxholes without him.

The time came for him to be sent home, and once again he was called before his officers. "We've called you in to see if you'd be willing to miss this boat and catch the next one in 10 days. If you will, we'll make you a sergeant."

"No, sir," Claudie replied, "I don't care about being a sergeant. Besides, just as soon as I get home I'm getting out of the service. It's my turn, and I'm going."

Once on ship he met another soldier who had left camp right after him. "It sure was good you made the choice you did, Doc, because a mortar round landed on your jeep and tore it to bits. Didn't leave nothing."

Within three years after Claudie returned from Korea, his mother, father, two sisters and two brothers, his wife's mother, her two brothers and sister, and the sister's husband, joined Claudie and his wife in the Adventist church.

It was safer in no-man's-land with Claudie than in the foxholes without him.

Claudie is God's friend. It's a simple, uncomplicated relationship. "In Korea, I could reach out and put my arms around Him anytime I wanted to."

Yes, Claudie is transparent. A person can see right through him to God's throne.

The Children Nobody Wanted

Her dark eyes sparkle with such liveliness and warmth you know immediately that Louise Emser loves people. Especially little people. As she watched four of her own grow up, this energetic grandmother couldn't bear the thought of living in a house without children. When she saw a notice in the newspaper about foster parenting, she knew she'd discovered a way to keep young ones in her house. So she called the welfare office, applied, and was accepted as a foster parent.

During the past 26 years 46 children have shared her heart and her home, staying anywhere from several months to a year or more. Three of them, now 26, 35, and 36 years of age, have been with her since they were little tykes. They are her family.

Of these special children, children nobody else wanted, 43 were handicapped in some way, either physically, mentally, or emotionally. But in Mrs. Emser each found someone to love and be loved by.

One of her first babies arrived at her door sick to the point of death with a severe stomach disorder. In addition to being mentally retarded, it was apparent she had never been properly cared for. She was rushed to the hospital where she would have died that night had it not been for the loving care of the doctor. She lived with Mrs. Emser for almost seven years before being put in a home for retarded children. Mrs. Emser still sees her.

Then there was 7-year-old Mary (not her real name). By the time she got to Mrs. Emser, she had been in 14 different homes. The report from the social services office said Mary couldn't learn, that she'd failed first grade. Mrs. Emser did the only thing she knew to do. She loved her and cared for her.

When school started the next fall, Mary was enrolled. Louise nervously waited out the first few weeks. She knew her little Mary, and she knew she could learn. But what if Mary's teacher didn't know it? What if the kids teased the little girl? What if school just plain frightened her?

She needn't have worried. Not only did Mary pass first grade, but the teacher said she couldn't tell any difference between her and the other children. Sad to say, she later went to a different home where she didn't do so well.

Eventually Mary came back to Mrs. Emser and had to start all over again. She's now married and has two children of her own. "She's a good mother," Mrs. Emser says with satisfaction.

Sometimes the children who came were so dirty she couldn't even comb their hair. But that was on the outside; with a little work it could be easily remedied. What was on the inside, the wounds of the heart, was a different matter.

She remembers two little brothers who came to her one September. Their mother was in the hospital and there was no one to care for the boys. They stood in Mrs. Emser's kitchen, thin little waifs with big eyes, looking at a bowl of oranges on the table. The smaller boy turned to his brother. "Baxter," he said, "I thought you said we couldn't have any oranges until Christmas."

"That almost broke my heart," Mrs. Emser says.

When they went home, a big bag of oranges went with them.

What is the hardest thing Mrs. Emser ever had to do? Even though it happened more than 20 years ago, you can still hear the pain in her voice. A mother loves all her children, but sometimes there is that certain child who tangles up the heartstrings hopelessly. Pat was such a baby. She came to Mrs. Emser when she was only 13 months old. Her father was in the service, stationed overseas, and her mother simply didn't take care of her. She wasn't potty trained, didn't talk much, and was just beginning to walk. For more than a year Mrs. Emser kept this baby, loving her and being loved back as only a child can love.

Then the social services decided to send the child back to her natural mother. "I remember praying, 'I don't think I can give this one up.'"

A mother loves all her children, but sometimes there is that certain child who tangles up the heartstrings hopelessly.

35

In those days, social service agencies did not allow the mothers to visit their children in the foster homes. So the change from foster home to original home was an abrupt one. The baby was confused and would have nothing to do with her mother.

"There was a real battle in my heart," Mrs. Emser admits. "I wanted that precious child. How I wanted her! I was almost glad when she cried for me. But I knew what I had to do. I talked the social services into letting the mother come into my home and I began teaching Pat to love her mother. And all the time it was breaking my heart.

"I told the mother to bring grapes when she came. Pat loved grapes."

From time to time Mrs. Emser would see the baby and her mother in the grocery store. "The baby would hold out her arms, but I couldn't take her. Giving her up was the hardest thing I ever did in my life."

Mrs. Emser didn't start driving until she was 67, after her husband passed away. Then the Lord blessed her with a car, and she knew that if she was going to be able to keep on doing the things she enjoyed doing, she'd have to learn to drive it.

"The people down at the license bureau and I got well acquainted since I was in there three times before I finally passed the test." She chuckles, remembering. "I'm still a chicken, but I do drive all the time."

Mrs. Emser keeps a schedule that would wear out a person considerably younger than her 80 years. She keeps a large garden and does most of her own yard work. Though she no longer takes in foster children, she still has children in the house. She kept a great-granddaughter and a great niece for more than a year. Presently she is taking care of the little daughter of a policewoman while she's at work. The money this single mother would normally have to pay for child care is used to keep her little girl in church school.

In addition to caring for her 83-year-old crippled brother, Mrs. Emser takes full care of her three foster sons. One of them suffers from spina bifida and requires special shoes, braces, and a walker. Without them he would be bedfast. From time to time the braces and shoes need to be replaced. And that's a very expensive worry. "But the Lord impresses me what to do. It's working out." People sometimes tell Mrs. Emser they couldn't do what she's doing. "I haven't done anything extra," she protests. "God has given me help; give Him the credit. Somebody has to help these people. Sometimes I lie in my comfortable bed at night in my warm house and think about the people out there. It makes me feel bad. What can one person do?

"Then I think, if God wants me to help, He'll provide the way. God's been so good to me. If I can make life a little better for others, that's what I'm here for. I've been blessed more than they have."

And so she has.

The Barefoot Hitchhiker

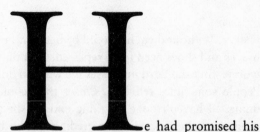

He had promised his children and grandchildren that he would not pick up any more hitchhikers. But there was something about the old man walking down Interstate 81 in his stocking feet, carrying his shoes. How dangerous could someone with sore feet be? James reasoned.

The man climbed into the car wearily, gratefully. He'd been on the road for a couple days, he said, and the rides hadn't been all that good. He'd been living in the South where he'd found work and a bed, but then he'd gotten a hankering to see his 2-year-old daughter again.

The baby's mother? Well, they weren't actually married. In fact, they'd had something of a fight before he left mother and child to find work. But it was springtime now, and he'd gotten a little lonesome. He thought he'd go home.

Mile after mile they rode through the Shenandoah Valley. "Where is home?" James asked finally.

"Up near Harrisburg, Pennsylvania."

"Well, I'll be able to get you as far as I-66, my turnoff," James told him. "I'm heading to Washington, D.C., to spend a few weeks with my grandchildren, and I turn east at Front Royal."

The man slid down a bit on the seat. "I think I'll take a little nap before I hit the pavement again. Wake me before you're ready to turn, will you?"

In the distance dogwood bloomed on the hillsides. It was early afternoon when James looked at his watch, considering. A side trip to Harrisburg? How far would that be out of the way? He shook his head as he passed the turnoff at Front Royal. His passenger slept on.

More than an hour passed. James touched the man's shoulder gently. "We're getting close to Harrisburg. You've got to tell me how to get to your place."

James pressed a few dollars into the man's hands as they said goodbye, and wished him well. He was eager to be on his way. It was getting late and he had a full hundred miles to go before he'd reach D.C.

Did the man patch up things with his girlfriend/wife? Was his baby daughter happy to see him? Did she even remember him? Was he able to find work in Pennsylvania?

A brief encounter. It took a little gas, a little energy, a little time—and a bit of the same love that Christ expressed when He walked barefoot on the hot, dusty roads of Palestine.

Swap Meet Pastor

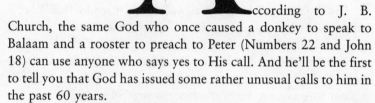

ccording to J. B. Church, the same God who once caused a donkey to speak to Balaam and a rooster to preach to Peter (Numbers 22 and John 18) can use anyone who says yes to His call. And he'll be the first to tell you that God has issued some rather unusual calls to him in the past 60 years.

Raised on a farm near Lubbock, Texas, he joined his parents in the Baptist Church when he was 12. Then just before he turned 13, his parents became Sabbathkeepers. He remembers well the April day in 1931 when his dad pushed the Model T Ford out of the barn and cranked it up. They drove the 16 miles into Lubbock to attend church, and that afternoon the three of them—mother, father, and son—were baptized in the cold water of a little lake in the city park.

Soon after, Elder B. E. Wagner came to town for a whole week to conduct a colporteur institute. Somehow, J.B. was allowed to attend that institute; he promised himself he would become a book and Bible salesperson as soon as possible. For two years he practiced his speech and read the books he hoped to sell someday.

One day, in response to an invitation he read in the conference colporteur newsletter, he hitchhiked to Dallas to attend another colporteur institute. He was ready to sell books and do justice to some of that good food they'd talked about in the invitation. Dressed in blue overalls and farm-boy shoes, his big cowboy hat in one hand and a homemade briefcase in the other, the 15-year-old received full attention when he walked into the meeting.

Looking back on it now, he can understand the concern in Brother Wagner's voice when he said, "I believe you are the youngest full-time colporteur I have ever met."

Nevertheless, for the next three years J.B. reported an average of 40 hours every week to the Texas Conference, hitchhiking across the Texas farmland with a briefcase full of books and Bibles. Wherever he found himself when the sun went down, he'd bargain with the farmer for room and board, offering a discount on the books the farmer bought in exchange.

He eventually moved back home, taking a job in the newspaper office while he finished high school. Then he went off to college where he fell in love with Hazel. They married and started their lives together in what would be 40 years of gospel ministry.

They retired in 1983 and began thinking about what they'd like to do next. God had been good. It might be nice to travel, visit the kids and grandkids. Maybe visit old friends and some camp meetings, sing a happy song. But that wasn't enough, somehow.

"When I was ordained," J.B. says, "I don't remember hearing anything about 'till retirement do we part.'"

So J.B. and Hazel began exploring different possibilities for a ministry that would combine their love of evangelism and travel, a kind of "mobile ministry." They prayed about it. They knocked on doors and visited trailer parks and neighborhoods, rich and poor. Throughout 1984 and 1985 they experimented with a health fair approach at the San Bernardino Swap Meet and a musical/preaching program in the city park. The good results they were hoping for just weren't forthcoming.

J.B. and his team decided they needed a whole new approach. Surveys he had read indicated that more than 50 percent of people in America claim they are Christians, but they don't attend church regularly nor do they have plans to attend. Here was his mission field! Nonchurch attenders need Christian fellowship, he reasoned. They need spiritual care and the good news about Jesus Christ. If they wouldn't or couldn't come to church, he'd bring church to them. Their methods, J.B. decided, would be the same ones used by the early Christian church: simple, personal, Christ-centered, trusting God for the results.

The San Bernardino Swap Meet is a big open air market. Every Sunday morning more than 1,000 vendors set up a complete city for the 10,000 to 15,000 buyers who come every week, then they take it away again about 3:00 p.m.

J.B. and his group rented a location. He built a mobile chapel on an 18-foot trailer that is bigger than the old Winnebago he uses to pull it around. The chapel looks like a church and is identified by a cross above its door. When they drive into the swap meet, people know they are there.

The Churches and their six regular team members arrive at the swap meet about 7:30 every Sunday morning. They've divided the swap meet into five districts, under the care of J.B., Herbert Church, Harold Kroetz, Phyllis Potts, and Jim Larson. To each one of these team members is assigned about 400 vendors. They distribute the weekly edition of the *Good News* paper and visit and pray with each of their "parishioners." They are with the people, sharing their joys, weeping when they weep, hurting when they hurt.

> "Don't let anyone tell you that nonchurch attenders don't want a pastor or that the world is so wicked that people have forgotten God."

"Don't let anyone tell you that nonchurch attenders don't want a pastor or that the world is so wicked that people have forgotten God. That just isn't so! People are crying for help. They keep coming to us," J.B. says.

The ministry has grown in the past six years. Consistency and dedication built confidence. Seven volunteer pastors talk to about 2,000 vendors, face to face, every Sunday. "Our team has been on the job every week. We see the same people every week. We know them; they know us. It took two years to really become established as the Swap Meet Pastor," J.B. says. "Printed sermons and other aids help, but most ministry is accomplished by dedicated Christians who give of themselves, not literature."

Every week the team members distribute 1,000 copies of the day's sermon. They could distribute 5,000 if they could afford to print that many. Some of the Christian swap meet vendors have become involved in the ministry by conducting Bible classes for the children. The video Bible story for the day, as told by the Swap Meet Pastor, is repeated every 15 minutes in the mobile chapel. A sign out front tells what is "now showing."

They've organized volunteer prayer groups, telephone prayer partners, potluck occasions and picnics, and other social activities.

Their special goal for 1990 was "small group ministries" for off-campus people. It has grown to 32 small groups that include 206 families. Some of their small-group leaders are already conducting Bible classes in homes.

"There are hundreds of areas that are open for a personal ministry such as ours," J.B. says. "There should be a local volunteer pastor for nonchurch attenders on every street, in every mobile home park, retirement center, and apartment complex. You don't need equipment! Just say 'Hello, there! I'm the volunteer pastor for nonchurch-attending Christians in this area. Do you know of Christian people who live near you who don't have a regular pastor? I would count it an honor to have your name on our free mailing list.' "

J.B. and Hazel are no longer trying to start a ministry—they are trying to find a little time to rest now and then between weddings, funerals, hospital calls, and all the other responsibilities that go with pastoral care. What a retirement!

The Attic Room

As I listened to her talk, I thought of the story of the Shunemite woman and her husband and wondered if the woman of Shunem had had the same laughter in her voice, bubbling over and around words she couldn't say fast enough.

As in the case of that long-ago woman, many a stranger has found his way down the dirt road that runs by the farm home of Jeannette and Russell Wilbur, though these strangers have not been prophets and their helpers.

Who are these people? Why do they come? Where do they come from?

Mrs. Wilbur laughs delightedly at my questions. "All kinds of people! Some of them just need a retreat, a place to get away for a while. Others are honeymooners with no family to share this special time of their lives and no place to go. And sometimes we have school children by the classroomful, maybe on a field trip to Niagara Falls, who need a place to stay."

"But why do they come to you?" I persist. "And how long do they stay?"

"The Lord sends them to us," Jeannette says simply, "and they stay as long as they need to."

The Wilburs' family philosophy of "open heart, open home" is a continuation of what she grew up with in her parents' home. Although Russell didn't grow up in a house like that, he readily adopted the idea and found himself caught up in the excitement of never knowing who might be sitting in his living room when he came home at night.

The three Wilbur children accepted the idea of sharing their bedrooms with these people whom the Lord "sent" as a way of life, and more than once cheerfully took up temporary sleeping

44

quarters on the living room sofa.

Sixteen-year-old Shirley showed up at one of the Wilburs' Saturday night socials at the invitation of a friend. When she got home, she asked her foster mother about these Adventists. "Only thing I know about Advents is that they keep Sunday for Monday," she was told.

Undeterred, Shirley kept coming back. Soon she was drawn into the swarm of young people that always surrounded the Wilburs. At first, Shirley kept her distance. Frankly, Mrs. Wilbur, tall and outgoing with an everywhere-at-once presence, intimidated her. Besides, people who would choose a building site *because* it was next to a schoolyard filled with yelling kids were a little scary, in Shirley's view.

Then one day Shirley and Mrs. Wilbur had a "run-in" and Shirley went home in great anger. After a time, the phone rang. "Let's talk about it," Mrs. Wilbur invited. "Come on down to the house." Even though it's been more than 25 years since that conversation took place, Shirley can't talk about it without great emotion.

"Jeannette Wilbur spent four and one half hours with me. With *just me!* She wanted to know who I was, my background, what I was going to do with my life. I became an Adventist because of her. She gave me seven years of loving counsel and tutoring, then I had a love experience with the Lord."

By this time Shirley was a regular member of the group of young people from non-Adventist homes invited to the Wilburs' for Sabbath dinner. Then dinner turned into afternoon activities and Saturday night fun, until most Saturdays she didn't get home before midnight. She had never experienced anything like this before. It was wonderful!

Shirley lived with the Wilburs, off and on, for more than 20 years. "To me, they're Mom and Dad. They've taught me what it means to experience God's love." She smiles wryly. "I've raked them over the coals and they still hold me dear to their hearts. The Wilburs showed me what God is like."

Since 1986 Shirley has been a valued employee at an Advent-

"The Wilburs showed me what God is like."

ist publishing house many miles from Holland, New York. But if you ask her where home is, you'll get only one answer.

In 1975 the Wilburs moved back to the old home place where Jeannette had grown up to help care for her ailing father. The house was too full of her parents' things to accommodate a second household of furniture, so Jeannette said, "Let's move into the barn! I've always loved it there."

And that's what they did. Mrs. Wilbur had soon transformed it into a cozy home, decorated in blue velvet and lace. Their dining room table stood on the spot where as a girl she used to milk the cow. It was a delightful place, quiet and private, warm and comfortable. After her father passed away and they moved into the house with Grandma Richards, she still went there to write and think and pray—when it wasn't being used by the people the Lord sent, that is.

Matthew Ma, the distant relative of a family friend, arrived from China in August 1989. The Wilburs helped him get settled at a nearby university where he is studying for his master's degree. A few months later, his girlfriend, who is also working on her degree, arrived. When Mrs. Wilbur learned they wanted to be married, she planned a Christmas wedding, complete with a catered dinner for 28. She borrowed a dress for the little bride, and Grandma Richards made the veil. And the barn/guest cottage? That was their honeymoon retreat!

It is no surprise that this young couple consider the Wilburs' house their home. That's the first place they came when they got their new driver's licenses. Nor is it a surprise that they wish to make the Wilburs' religion their own.

As the Wilbur children grew up and moved away, Mrs. Wilbur turned the bedrooms into guest rooms. At present, one of these rooms is occupied by a young woman who came to them more than a year ago. When Mrs. Wilbur answered the phone that January day, a voice asked if she knew of someone who could provide a "house jail" for a 25-year-old woman inmate.

It was the first time in the history of Western New York that the prison authorities had been faced with the dilemma of having to trust a prisoner out of their sight and direct care, but this woman was due to deliver a baby in a few days. What was she charged with? Mrs. Wilbur asked. She had been at the scene of a murder and was considered a suspect in the case.

Mrs. Wilbur knew what she was being asked to do. And she knew Who was asking her to do it, but she told the caller she didn't know of anyone who could help, and hung up. For four days she struggled with the idea, resisting, but in the end she said, "Thank You, Father," and made arrangements for the new guest.

So in January 1990 Rin came to the Wilburs' house and settled in upstairs. The baby that was due in a few days didn't arrive for five weeks. "The Lord wanted Rin out of jail and able to rest," Mrs. Wilbur says. After the baby was born, Rin exhibited such good behavior that the authorities allowed her to stay on in the Wilburs' home.

Not until she came to the Wilburs' did Rin discover that meek people are not weak people. Because of the violent environment in which she had grown up, this was a new concept. She immersed herself in her hosts' joy of living. The time came when she had to know why they could be so happy and how she could find it for herself.

"Russell and I have known a lot of cheerful people and are that way ourselves, but Rin is the most cheerful person we've met. She may cry herself to sleep, but she doesn't inflict her tragedy on anyone. And that baby!" Mrs. Wilbur's voice swells with a grandmother's pride. "He's 9 months old and walking! Loves to be picked up and hugged."

No one knows what the future holds for Rin and her small son. But God does, and He is Rin's personal Friend.

In June 1990 Grandma Richards passed away. She never had any pain; she just wore out. For most of her 95 years this house had been filled with her gentle presence. Here she had taught her children by her example the adventure of opening their hearts and homes to God's children.

An adventurer to the end, at the age of 90 she decided to walk the 70 miles to the house in which she had been born. The

> Mrs. Wilbur knew what she was being asked to do. . . . For four days she struggled with the idea, resisting.

newspapers, happy to have something good to talk about, monitored her progress carefully, giving daily reports during the two weeks it took her to complete her journey. And now the sun-drenched corner bedroom was empty. So empty.

But not for long. Four months later, Mrs. Wilbur made Grandma's room over for John. How hard it was! Each change she made seemed to stab at the emptiness in her heart. But John was their neighbor—literally, not just in the good Samaritan sense. Legally blind and quite deaf, John had been told after a recent operation that he would have to find someone to live with or else go to a nursing home. Knowing that a nursing home would kill a man of John's spirit, the Wilburs took him in.

Never married, John is an inventor who has lived his life with his machinery. He may be 86, but he's not ready to quit yet. He works in his own shop, which is equipped with every machine imaginable. His creative brain is still turning out inventions. (He has one invention being considered in the patent office right now; it is a window that doesn't need glazing.) Russell Wilbur has become a sort of chauffeur to the elderly man, driving him from his country home to his city home, running his errands.

Sometimes he yells at Mrs. Wilbur when she forgets to do something, but the storm lasts only a brief moment. "He's been a commander, you know," Mrs. Wilbur defends him, "running his own shop. He's an absolute delight. We've come a long way," she laughs, "because he's allowing me to clean up both his houses . . ." She pauses. "How shall I say it? They really look like bachelor's quarters, but it's so much fun! I can really see my progress. I just pick at it whenever I have a few minutes. He would never allow anyone in before, but by spring we will have open house for the neighbors."

"Saturday night we had a Christmas party for him," she continues. "It was a surprise!" (When she chuckles I wonder who had the most fun.) "Eight of his city friends came and enjoyed a meal and took turns pumping the player piano. Of course, there were presents for everybody, and then we sat in front of John and just talked to *John.*"

. . . .

Knowing that a nursing home would kill a man of John's spirit, the Wilburs took him in.

John enjoyed himself thoroughly, but his face wore a sort of lost look. "Why are you doing this?" he asked finally.

Mrs. Wilbur knelt in front of him so he could hear. "Because you are special."

The old man's eyes clouded over. "I've tried to be special to someone all of my life, but it just never happened," he said.

God has not been important in John's life. "He's always been so self-sufficient he hasn't needed God," Mrs. Wilbur explains.

However, at the Wilburs' house where they pray about everything, it's hard to avoid God. When he had some bad spots on his legs that required frequent fomentation treatments, Mrs. Wilbur would hold John's feet in her lap before beginning the treatment and pray for them. One of the spots has healed completely, and the others are getting better, she reports. Not long ago, as John was leaving for town to deal with tough lawyers regarding some lawsuits, he paused at the door. "Maybe we better pray about this," he said.

John has moved warily from the rough and tumble business world where "greedy hands are trying to weasel my money out of me" to this gentle home where he is loved and accepted and not charged a cent. He must be forgiven if he keeps looking for the catch.

One evening at worship each person was expressing what he had to be thankful for. John's turn came. His eyes lit up as he looked around the circle of faces that has grown so dear to him. In his heavy German accent he said, "I tink I struck it rich!"

Like the man and woman of Shunem, the Wilburs thought to do a kindness "when they built the room on the roof of their house," but the kindness has come back to them, as it always does.

Hurting
Hearts

It was the final meeting of a women's weekend retreat, and Kay Kuzma was challenging her audience of more than 200 to listen to God's call to ministry. "I strongly believe that God has a special ministry for everyone," she told them. "There is a wonderful feeling of fulfillment that comes when you follow God's calling."

After the meeting two women asked her if a retreat could be planned for women with hurting childhoods, specifically for those who were victims of incest and sexual abuse.

"Let's pray that God will call someone to lead this retreat," Kay responded.

Minutes later Marty (not her real name) approached her saying she wanted to talk about what God was calling her to do. She said she felt her training and life experiences would allow her to work with cancer victims, drug and alcohol abusers, or marriage separation and renewal.

"Have you had incest in your background?" Kay interrupted.

Marty was shocked. She never talked about this topic or her offender, now dead, who had not been a member of the Christian community. "Yes," she stammered, "but God has helped me to completely forgive the offender."

Suddenly Kay was impressed to ask, "Would you be willing to lead out in a retreat for women with hurting childhoods, such as incest?"

Marty hesitated. "Yes," she said finally, "but let me pray about it."

Ever since she had moved into the area six months before, Marty had been praying for a ministry, but it seemed no one needed her. Even though she was a registered nurse and held credentials in rehabilitative counseling, she couldn't find a job. In

50

church and in her Bible study group, she kept asking God what He wanted her to do. Her spiritual gifts test showed that she was strong in the areas of faith, wisdom, and teaching, but no opportunity to use these gifts had presented itself. About that time she read about the Designing God's Woman Seminar and felt impressed to attend. She had no idea she would be faced with this painful dilemma.

At home that night she fell on her knees in prayer. "I don't want this mission," she pleaded.

I'll go where you want me to go, echoed a voice in her mind. "My wound is too great!"

There is a balm in Gilead.

Sobs shook her body. "I just want to be home with You and forget the pain."

But what of My other hurting children?

When she cried out, "I'm not strong enough for this mission," she heard, *I can do all things through Jesus who strengthens me.*

She continued to agonize, but all she could think of was Jonah. "I surely don't want to end up in a whale's belly!"

When her son called her the next night, she shared her dilemma with him. "Mom, ask God for a sign," he advised. So she asked God that if He wanted her to work in this ministry, to send a woman to her who would ask for help in the area of incest. She gave Him a week, even though she wanted to say 24 hours!

The next morning in her spiritual fellowship recovery group she shared that she was trying to turn her life and will over to God for a ministry and wanted to "let go and let God" work in her life. She gave no further information.

After the meeting, a woman walked up to Marty and shared that she too wanted to let God work in her life. Then a strange look came over her face. "You're an incest survivor, aren't you?" she said.

Shaken, Marty replied, "Yes, but God has given me peace and love for the offender."

The woman reached out her hand. "Would you help me?" She went on to explain that her father (the offender) was gravely ill.

The woman reached out her hand. "Would you help me?"

51

Because she didn't want to visit him, her family was angry with her.

God had given Marty her answer in just 12 hours. She was being called to minister to women with hurting childhoods—specifically those who had survived incest and sexual abuse.

For more than a year Marty has been conducting a program for women who have been damaged in their childhood and who now long to find healing. Her goal is to provide an environment for women to come together in a safe, anonymous, Christian-sponsored weekend to meet sister survivors, process some feelings in groups, and have spiritual prayer sponsors available if a woman desires this. Women who are incest/sexual abuse survivors are the only persons attending these workshops. In an effort to maintain complete privacy and anonymity, they are known only by their first names.

There are so many women—and men—who are dying inside, maybe not even realizing that it was abuse in childhood that has caused them to be so confused about life. It has been estimated that one fourth of the women in America (more than 34 million) and one in seven of the men have experienced childhood sexual abuse.

"But a more startling fact," Marty says, "is that a great majority of those women were raised (and abused) in 'conservative Christian' homes.

"Every hour more than 30 children are sexually abused by a parent, parental figure, sibling, or other family member. I have a belief that Satan, the great perpetrator of evil, attacks when children are very young to harm their relationship with God."

It takes courage to speak out on an issue as sensitive as incest. And it takes courage to seek help. A common thread of fear among women who have been victims of sexual abuse is their difficulty in even writing and asking for help.

But they are reaching out, responding, learning to let go of their feelings of shame and guilt. Is it difficult? Yes! Is it painful? Yes! For both the workshop participants and the directors.

"Before each workshop I go through it all again," Marty says.

> For Marty, following God's plan means working in an area that she had hoped could be buried forever.

"All the doubts are back. I wonder, Will I be able to do this? Will I be able to show God's love, assure them they can be restored to Jesus? Am I the right person for this? And each time the Lord affirms me in some way, and I go ahead."

But it leaves her drained, exhausted. For Marty, following God's plan means working in an area that she had hoped could be buried forever. Every time she dips into her painful past to try to help others, it hurts. Those awful memories are still there.

But so is the healing. She, and those to whom she ministers, can be whole again, just like the woman who reached out and touched the hem of Jesus' robe. His promise to her is also theirs: "Daughter, be of good comfort; thy faith hath made thee whole" (Matthew 9:22).

(If you would like more information on this ministry, you may write to: Family Matters, Box 2222, Redlands, California 92373.)

No Crowds
for Me!

o, partner, no, I don't think I can go with you. Too many people! And wherever there's a lot of people, there's a lot of drinking, cursing, and fighting. Thanks, but no thanks!"

Jesse Duncan, tall and soft-spoken, always smiling, smoothed out imaginary wrinkles in his black chauffeur's uniform as he refused his brother-in-law's invitation to go with him to camp meeting.

The two men were good friends. They genuinely liked each other. But this time Edward was asking a little too much. It wasn't that Jesse didn't like to travel. As a chauffeur he was on the road more than he was at home. No, traveling wasn't the problem— crowds of people were.

As a chauffeur Jesse spent most of his time in the company of only one person, his employer. And in order to drive according to his employer's expectations, Jesse had to keep his attention focused. ("Jesse, I never want to feel the car stop," were the old man's exact words.) There was little conversation between them. So crowds weren't something Jesse felt comfortable with.

Edward, on the other hand, was talkative and outgoing, never meeting a stranger. He thrived on being around many people. The more the better. He wanted his brother-in-law to enjoy what he had been enjoying for a long time—camp meeting. If only he could get Jesse to go. But how?

Then he had an idea. Jesse loved to dress well. Bought the best brand-name suits. Edward approached Jesse again. "I'll make a deal with you. You go with me to camp meeting, and if you see anyone drinking, if you hear anyone cursing, or if you see anyone fighting while we're there, I'll get you the best suit of clothes money can buy. Now, you know I'm a man of my word. If you see even one person doing any of those things, you've got a brand-new suit of clothes. Deal?"

"But I smoke," Jesse objected.

"That's OK," Edward answered. "When you want to smoke I'll take you some place away from the campground. No problem. Is it a deal?"

Jesse considered for a moment, then said, "OK, partner, it's a deal. I'll go."

The next Sabbath they drove to Pine Forge, Pennsylvania, for camp meeting. The car threaded its way out of the mountains to the valley floor, which was carpeted with acres of tents that were populated by thousands of people. Jesse looked around nervously, but said nothing. Edward took him to meetings, introduced him to many people, showed him all around. Late in the day Jesse asked Edward to take him somewhere "so I can smoke."

They took the narrow asphalt road leading away from the campground into the surrounding hills and parked the car. There was a long silence as they looked down at the camp spread out below. Jesse was pensive, but he didn't smoke.

After a while he spoke. "Partner, what kind of people are these? No smoking, no drinking, no cursing, no fighting. Everybody's happy. What kind of people are these?"

They returned from camp meeting late that Saturday night. Not much talking was done.

Two weeks later Jesse approached his brother-in-law. "I want to go to church with you next Sabbath, partner," he said matter-of-factly.

Edward doesn't remember what the sermon was about that Sabbath some 17 years ago. But he does remember that when the invitation was given to join the church, his brother-in-law, Jesse Duncan, walked forward.

The man who was afraid of crowds. The man who thought that a gathering of many people brought only fighting, cursing, and drinking. The man who wanted to know "what kind of people are these" accepted a deal and became a part of "those

There was a long silence as they looked down at the camp spread out below.

people," and was baptized into the Seventh-day Adventist Church. Jesse may have lost a fine suit of clothes, but he won a robe of righteousness.

Walking by Galilee

No doubt about it. The Harmons (not their real name) are a committed Christian family. They firmly believe in their church and its mission. *So does everyone else in my church,* you're thinking. However, the way the Harmons have chosen to act on these beliefs sets them apart.

Their idea of ministry is not so much something a person *does* once a week as something he *lives,* something he shares. Their philosophy of ministry is doing the thing that is right beside you. Doing what lies in your path.

"If you have to drive across town to do missionary work, it doesn't get done," Mrs. Harmon says. "Start with the people close by—your neighbors. Become involved."

Not many people are thinking about church mission and witnessing possibilities when they purchase a home. As the real estate people say, the three most important things to remember in buying a home are location, location, location. The Harmons couldn't agree more. But not for the usual reason!

When they bought their present house, it was a run-down Victorian in the underprivileged part of town and in need of everything. Maybe the investment potential was there, but more importantly, the location of their new home allowed them to live with and share the concerns of the people to whom they wished to minister. Having done this twice before in other communities, they had learned that once a person can stop thinking of himself as God's gift to the neighborhood, he is free to join in on the good things that are already happening there.

Because of their interest in the preservation of old houses and the environment, they've restored their house, creating jobs in the process by using as many local people as show themselves able to participate in the project. Probably as many as 25 people worked

57

on their present home, including eight to ten young people. Carpenters, painters, landscapers, maintenance people—all worked together with the Harmons, developing skills and gaining experience.

The biggest plus, though, is the opportunity for the mixing of two cultures. For some people, insulated in the close cocoon of their small town, this mixing is a first look at an unthought-about world, a kaleidoscope of new experiences. At first they know nothing about each other, but gradually they change, in such a way that they really don't know they're mixing. It just happens. Naturally.

Each morning the work force meets with Mrs. Harmon in her "executive office," which is a picnic table under a big tree in the backyard. There they have planning sessions and analyze their work and mistakes. They discuss work not done, appointments not kept. They make daily decisions and assignments, evaluating work in a hands-across-the-table atmosphere.

The tone of the meeting is matter-of-fact and low-key, open, nonaccusatory, and professional. Each knows he is responsible for his own actions, tools, and supplies. This is a totally new exposure that even school does not give. People see each other on good days and bad days. When setbacks occur, they learn to handle it without becoming abrasive or violent (a good thing to know in this particular neighborhood!).

There's a neighborhood block picnic each summer in somebody's backyard. At Christmas Mrs. Harmon and her neighbors get together and make Christmas wreaths out of live greens. In spring they plan what flowers they will plant around their homes. As a result the neighborhood looks lovely, artistic, and co-ordinated. That's nice; but getting together is the important part.

An avid antique buff, Mrs. Harmon is always on the lookout for someone else's junk from which to make a treasure. As she drives by a lamp shop one day she notices what looks like a couple of usable lamp shades in the trash bin. She takes them home, washes them, and gives them away. The next time she's in the shop, she tells the owner about it.

> For some people, insulated in the close cocoon of their small town, this mixing is a first look at an unthought-about world, a kaleidoscope of new experiences.

"Do you know of other people who need lamp shades?" the lady asks. "I have some leftovers I can't get rid of."

"Some" turns out to be almost 30!

Mrs. Harmon has involved herself in the politics of the small town, attending commission meetings, sending letters, marching for good causes. She takes part in historic open houses as a way to generate civic pride.

She's involved with the town's homesteading program. Tax reversion properties, wonderful old homes that require a lot of work to bring them up to city code, are available for $1 each to any qualified citizens who will improve them in a stated length of time. Even a person on welfare can apply for one of these homes—credit history is a more important factor than income. (A person with good credit is one who has consistently met his financial obligations on time.)

"In some ways we live in a typical small town," Mrs. Harmon says. "People walk a lot. And everybody knows when the fire truck leaves the firehouse because it practically goes by their front door."

As their house is on a busy street corner, the Harmons also experience things that aren't so typical. More than once the Harmon home has become a temporary asylum to neighbors, friends, and strangers being pursued by weapon-bearing people.

"It's been a full three years," Mrs. Harmon smiles, remembering. "When it comes to ministry, people are really generous at heart. They're willing to respond to a real need. Often it's just a matter of knowing how to plug in."

Goldsboro Hears a Sermon

The Goldsboro Adventist Church is probably not unlike a hundred other small churches across the country. Housed in a neat brick building tucked away in a tiny North Carolina town, it is the center of fellowship for the 35 members who attend week after week.

Polly Anderson was aware that when Flossie Worley read the mission story that Sabbath morning last summer, probably half of the members didn't catch most of it. Elderly and hard of hearing, they did hear enough to learn there were needy students in the Soviet Union and gladly gave their offerings to help.

As she walked home from church that day, Polly was troubled. She longed to do something for the dear people in her little church. They needed a lift, she decided, a personal, up-close look at what was going on in the church they had been so faithfully supporting all these years. But what could she do?

When her son, Elbert Anderson, Jr., called her that afternoon, he could tell she was depressed. "Our little church is so isolated. Nobody knows we're here. And right now we don't even have a preacher. How I wish we could have a *live* sermon! First class! Hear for ourselves what Adventists are doing in the world," she told him.

As the two of them continued to talk, Polly got an idea. She had just finished reading *Soviet Sonrise* (by Rose Otis, published by the Review and Herald Publishing Association) and had been greatly moved by what the book described was happening in the Soviet Union. It was a firsthand account she wanted, wasn't it? Why not invite this Elder Otis, the author's husband, who was closely connected with the new work in the Soviet Union, to speak to their little church?

"Right!" her son laughed.

60

"Maybe not in person," Polly insisted. "Maybe he'd talk to us by *phone*."

Many phone calls later, Polly found out that Elder Otis worked at the General Conference in Washington, D.C. Placing a call to the church's world headquarters, she told his secretary what she wanted.

"I'm sure she thought I was crazy," Polly laughed later, "but she was nice and sounded really sorry as she explained that it would be hard for me to talk to him even over the phone."

Polly assured her she didn't mind being put on hold while Elder Otis was located. And she kept holding until her patience was rewarded. When Elder Otis came on the line, Polly shared her dream with him. In her soft southern voice she told him about the lovely people in the Goldsboro church, of their love for the Lord and His children everywhere, of their longing to be a part of the exciting events they heard about in mission stories and books.

When he listened with such understanding, she boldly made her request: If Elder Otis couldn't visit their little church in person, would he be willing to bring them a message by *telephone?* Polly quickly outlined her plan to arrange for a speaker phone to be plugged in and amplified so everyone could *hear* his sermon live, even if they couldn't *see* him.

"I've never done anything like this before," Elder Otis told her, but the idea intrigued him. "You get everything together and I'll do it!" he promised.

Polly had only a few days to work on it because he was on his way to California and from there to the Soviet Union. Everywhere she turned, she faced more obstacles. The phone in the church office wouldn't reach to the small speakers in the church. When Polly explained her project to the people at the phone company, they seemed interested and sympathetic but told her it wouldn't work.

One of their employees, coming into the office to check out for the weekend, overheard her story. He suggested some ideas she could try.

But time was running out.

Sabbath morning she brought in a borrowed speaker phone. A retiree from the phone company fixed up a cord to reach from office to pulpit, and at three minutes before 11:00, Polly's phone was ready!

The people sat quietly, expectantly, watching the phone sitting on the wooden pulpit at the front of the church. Promptly at 11:00 it rang! Elder Otis was on the line, calling from a motel room in California. But three minutes later, the phone went dead. For 45 minutes, Elder Otis spoke, unaware that he wasn't getting through. But not a person in the Goldsboro church left. They waited quietly, hoping that somehow, some way the faraway voice would come through the speaker again.

The disappointment was almost too much to bear. D. J. Hill, a convert through a Revelation Seminar the church had held the year before, got through to Elder Otis's motel in California. He talked to eight people, including the manager, but no one seemed to be able to help. So he kept trying Elder Otis's room phone until he finally got through.

"How did it go?" Elder Otis asked.

"I'm afraid we didn't hear any of it," Polly replied, near tears.

"You didn't hear any of it? I've talked for 47 minutes!"

D.J. took the phone from Polly. "Not one person has left, Elder Otis. They have been sitting here praying that we would be able to get you back on the line." He paused. "I know we couldn't expect you to do it over again."

Elder Otis seemed as distressed as they, concerned over their long wait. "I'll be glad to do it over again," he assured them graciously.

And he did. This time his voice came strong and clear over the phone, as though he were in the room with them. They recorded the message on tape as he spoke.

Elder Otis told them about the new seminary near Moscow, and the gardens the students were learning to grow. He described the big cabbages and how the Soviets had learned to love corn, and the excitement these beautiful gardens were generating in the community. He spoke about plans for a new publishing house and

> The people sat quietly, expectantly, watching the phone sitting on the wooden pulpit at the front of the church.

of little children who had never seen a picture of Jesus.

Each person in the Goldsboro church heard every word, and for the next hour it was as though they were in the Soviet Union seeing these miracles with their own eyes.

The story doesn't end here. Word got around town about the unusual sermon, and Polly found herself sharing the taped message with her attorney, the phone company, and preachers from other churches. Her brother's social worker heard it and said she would have been in church that week had she known about it. She and her husband, an important businessman in town, have been coming to see Polly, wanting to know more about what Seventh-day Adventists believe.

Mr. Beasley, a mainstay of the Goldsboro church for more than 25 years, laughingly said he almost had a full-time ministry copying tapes for Polly to share. Tapes of that Sabbath morning sermon have been sent all over the country to bless and inspire those who receive them.

Two months later the Goldsboro members heard that Elder Otis and delegates from the Soviet Union were going to be in Charlotte, North Carolina, en route to the General Conference session in Indianapolis. D. J. Hill loaded as many people into his van as it would hold and headed for Charlotte.

"How will Elder Otis know us?" someone worried.

"We'll make a sign!" Norma Hill declared. Rummaging around in the back of the van she produced a large sheet of paper and they went to work on their message.

When he stepped out of the side room just before the meeting began, Elder Otis saw a group of happy people holding high a large sign that read: "Attention: Pastor Otis, We're your Goldsboro, NC, Telephone Friends!"

And that's how Elder Otis finally got to meet the people to whom he had given one of his most unusual sermons—not once, but twice!

What started out as a desire to bless and enrich a tiny church in North Carolina has proved to be a blessing to hundreds of people, including their brothers and sisters in the Soviet Union.

> **For the next hour it was as though they were in the Soviet Union seeing these miracles with their own eyes.**

63

Yes, the people in the Goldsboro church are very busy these days working on projects to help their fellow believers over there.

You never know what a difference one phone call and a little persistence can make!

The Get-Well Card

Billy Joe was a whiner. He worked in the Safeway Bread Plant factory, in the hot, rough world of heavy machinery, and was always nursing a new complaint.

"Look, Pauline, I burned my arm," he said one day as the office manager passed by his work station. "And last week I got soap in my eyes."

Laughter erupted around him. "Yup! Our resident crybaby burned his arm," the man working next to him mimicked.

Billy Joe was the joke of the factory, the object of ridicule, a man whose name was always good for a laugh. In that muscle-grinding world where men missed work because they were drunk or lazy, Billy Joe's frequent physical complaints fell on deaf ears. He didn't even know how to have a good time.

"Pauline, I don't have a friend in the whole world," he said to her one day. "I thought Jack was my friend, but I heard him talking about me. There isn't one person who likes me."

Pauline patted his arm. "Billy Joe, you have two good friends. I like you, and God loves you." After a few more words, she went on her way.

One morning Pauline walked into the lunchroom. The icy air felt good compared to the dry Texas heat that filled every nook of the big, noisy warehouse. Billy Joe was with a group of men who were leaving the little room, laughing and joking. As they passed Pauline, Billy Joe hung back.

"I don't know what to make of them," he told her. "They were laughing at me because I believe in God. You believe in God, don't you?"

They talked for a few minutes about God and His love and care.

Billy Joe didn't come to work one day. His wife called to say that he was in the hospital. This report brought a new round of jokes from the men, but Pauline went to her desk and picked out a get-well card from the stock she kept there.

"Don't tell me you're sending that professional sickie a get-well card!" one of the men hooted.

"Why not?" Pauline replied evenly. "I always keep a few in my desk."

Billy Joe died suddenly three days later. Placed carefully on the table next to his bed was the only get-well card he had ever received.

Walking on Air

The teenaged boys gathered in the gymnasium of the boys' reformatory were not ordinary kids. They shifted uneasily in their metal chairs, calling out now and then to the group of men on stage who were finishing a musical program.

Then Bill Church stepped to the mike and began speaking. The noise stopped abruptly. The stories he told about life in prison rang with the authority of someone who had been there, and these boys were definitely interested. Most of these 12- to 18-year-old boys were headed for prison.

Bill had been there. He assured them it was no place they wanted to be. Many of them heard for the first time about the freedom that comes with knowing Jesus. Bill treasures the letters he received from some of the boys, thanking him for speaking to them.

"Once you do something for the Lord, you can never *not* do anything again. You start looking for needs you can fill." Somehow you know the conviction you hear in Bill Church's voice comes from personal experience.

Bill's been filling needs for a long time now, and in the process he's made some exciting discoveries. He's discovered that most people would like to be involved in a ministry of service. Usually, all they need is a nudge in the right direction. "If you simply open your heart, you will be led into areas where you can be of service," he says.

Never one to keep a good thing to himself, Bill embarked on his adventure in service years ago and uncovered enough needs to keep a churchful of people busy.

Not long after he became the personal ministries leader of his local church, he discovered a stack of cards from the *It Is Written* telecast viewers who had requested visits. Even though the cards looked like they had lain around the church for a long time, Bill decided it would be a good project to start with. He divided the cards among the 15 or 20 volunteers who stayed after church. What happened next galvanized the church into action.

Harvey Michaels, one of the volunteers, stopped by the house indicated on his card. He introduced himself to the woman who answered the door and stated the reason for his visit.

"I wish you had been here six months ago," she said sadly. "My son committed suicide."

There was no shortage of volunteers after that. Making those visits had suddenly become a life and death matter. The cards were divided up according to areas where church members lived. That way, church families were visiting their neighbors, spending time with them.

The Pathfinders and young people regularly visited the nearby convalescent hospitals, singing and visiting with the patients. It was hard to tell who enjoyed it more—the old folks or the young people.

Bill's ministry took an interesting turn the night he went to hear a children's choir from Uganda. As an employee of Items, International Airwalk, the company that manufactures Airwalk shoes, he tends to notice what people are wearing on their feet. These children, who sang like angels, had on the most beat-up, run-down shoes Bill had ever seen. When he learned that arrangements had been made to take the kids to Disneyland, he determined they would go in style.

Back at his company, he rounded up shoes, shirts, hats, and jackets, all bearing the Airwalk logo. Those kids looked beautiful! One little 8-year-old, ecstatic over his new hightops, tried expressing himself in broken English, but soon gave that up for his native language. Even that wasn't enough. His feelings were beyond words.

The shoes—samples, seconds, and returns that would ordinarily be thrown away—soon found their way into a score of Bill's projects. A multi-denominational orphanage has received literally

> These children, who
>
> sang like angels, had
>
> on the most beat-up
>
> run-down shoes Bill had
>
> ever seen.

tons of them. Every summer when kids from a nearby academy go down to Mexico on a church-building project, they take along 25 to 30 cases (12 pairs of shoes in each case). Another 30 cases of shoes have found their way to an Indian reservation.

Bill takes shoes to a center for abused children in North San Diego, to orphanages, and to half a dozen other places where he knows they will be used. Every year, boys and girls around Hilo, Hawaii, get a new pair of shoes. In an area where the farm families often find it difficult to make a living, having shoes is a significant blessing.

Recently the director of a center for battered children brought a group of boys to the Airwalk warehouse. As they enthusiastically tried on shoes, Bill noticed a 15-year-old jumping up and down, unbelieving. "I've always wanted a pair of Airwalks!" he exclaimed happily. As any adolescent knows, shoes "make the man," and at this moment he was just like any other kid. He had been given more than a pair of shoes; he'd been given self-esteem.

Bill knows about being different. He had polio when he was young and remembers how the other kids singled him out because of his limp and the built-up shoes he had to wear.

"To know you've knocked a few rocks out of some kid's pathway . . . It doesn't get much better than that," he says.

His philosophy? Make the best of every day. Find something to do for somebody that will lighten that person's load. Do a deed, fill a need. And most important of all, speak to each person you meet as if his heart were breaking, because it just might be.

Speak to each person you meet as if his heart were breaking, because it just might be.

69

Throwaway Babies

George and Linda Groth's journey of joy was turning into a horrible nightmare. Scotty was under arrest. Mexican immigration officials declared he was an illegal alien and must be deported to Guatemala. He could expect to receive the same beans-and-bus-deportation regimen as other illegal aliens, but until then he must wait alone in a cold jail cell. That was a lot of trouble to be in, especially considering Scotty was only one week old.

The Groths had learned about Scotty's need for a home from self-supporting missionaries in Guatemala and had made arrangements for Linda to fly down and pick up the baby. All went well until she returned to the Calexico border with Scotty, where George and their three children waited in anxious anticipation.

The immigration officials became suspicious of this white woman with a brown baby and wouldn't let her through, instructing her to return the next morning. When her turn finally came, she was interrogated at length and subjected to extensive verbal abuse. Then she was read her rights and arrested.

George and the children knew none of this as they waited in their truck on the other side of the border. As the hours passed, George begged everyone passing by for information. Finally, one of the officers told him his wife was under arrest and would go to prison for five years.

Eventually, after a flurry of bargaining and pleading, Linda was released and George was given permission to take Scotty back to the missionaries in Guatemala. (The officials said they didn't want to be responsible for the baby's death in the jail cell.)

What followed was an 11-day ordeal in which George and Scotty shuttled back and forth from Mexicali to Guatemala City. Finally George flew back to his family in Los Angeles.

70

"We already felt that Scotty was our child, and when his adoption didn't work out, we felt such an emptiness," George says.

As time went by they wondered what to do to fill this emptiness. They felt an urge in their hearts to do some kind of good for the needy, but what? Both George and Linda are nurses; his specialty is in psychiatry. It occurred to them that perhaps they could minister to battered infants in their home area. So they applied to the county child protective services for a foster home license.

Within a few months they were licensed and received their first three children, all at once, just as they were leaving on a two-week vacation. They packed their suddenly-doubled family into their little Brat pickup camper. Their own children consisted of Jenny, 9; Jeff, 6; and Wendy, 5. The newcomers were aged 2, 18 months, and one month.

Back from vacation, George and Linda rented a huge old house and filled it with baby furniture and equipment. After about a year they decided to create a special kind of foster home—a crisis/emergency home. At any hour of the day or night, children would arrive at their door.

"We get a lot of drug-addicted babies," George says, "and many who have been starved and beaten. A few of them are toddlers and older kids, but most of them are infants."

This has grown into a family ministry that involves not only George and Linda, but their three teenage children and Linda's mother. Because of the great needs of their small charges, they never have more than six babies at one time. During the past 10 years they've ministered to more than 400 babies, keeping them from a few weeks to a few months, until they can be placed with a relative, foster parent, or returned to their own parents. Of the latter, some have been rehabilitated, some have not.

How do the Groths handle the rage they must feel when a tiny person who's been the object of terrible evil is left at their door?

"At first there is great vindictive anger," George admits. "But that doesn't do good for anybody. We have to recognize that the

71

abuser is a damaged person and we concentrate on doing what we can to make these babies' lives better."

These children are disenfranchised, George goes on to explain. They have no say in how they are to be treated. Many times they are returned to abusive homes. Since each case is completely confidential, no one is allowed to know what is going on. The welfare system is so overburdened and underfunded the kids can't be carefully protected.

"If only a law were passed to make hearings public so the media could go in and make judges and social workers accountable for their judgments, then the public could know if children are adequately protected."

Many judges and social workers are conscientious, but others are hardened and overworked. If the public could know what goes on, we could all look out for these children. Often parents are not even prosecuted. They are guilty of sexually abusing, starving, and beating their babies, yet they don't ever see a day in jail. The children can't vote or speak, and are under the direst threats to keep their terrible secret.

George says, "Almost every child who is killed at the hands of a parent or guardian has come to the attention of a child care person at one time or another, sometimes several times. We aren't adequately protecting them."

In all this bleakness, there are happy stories. George's voice vibrates as he tells his favorite success story. A woman became very angry with her husband and decided to get even with him by maiming or killing their 18-month-old baby. She gave him a bottle of gasoline, then wrapped his face in a gas-soaked rag. The toxicity of the gas burned holes in the baby's internal organs and his lungs were seared by the fumes.

The baby was rushed to Loma Linda University Medical Center, where the doctors' heroic efforts barely saved his life. He eventually recovered and was normal in every way except he had been permanently blinded. The doctors said he had suffered severe nerve damage and would never see again.

Almost six months later, a childless couple contacted the

county social agency, expressing their deep desire to adopt a little boy. The man had all the usual dreams of having a son to play ball with and take fishing, so when they were told about the little blind baby, they hesitated. Once they met him, however, he captured their hearts totally. For the first time in his young life, the little guy was loved completely and without reserve.

A few months later the baby miraculously regained his sight. Medically, it can't be explained. "Purely the power of love!" George exults.

As for the Groth family's plans for the future, George says they will keep right on doing what they are doing. "Most of us can't do much about the people who are starving in third world countries, but there is plenty of need right next door to us. Our babies come from every race, religion, and socio-economic classification. Their need knows no boundaries. We'll be here as long as they need us."

There are many wicked people in the world. On the other hand, there are at least as many saints. The saints are just more quiet. And in the case of the Groths, they are more determined.

. . . .

"Most of us can't do much about the people who are starving in third world countries, but there is plenty of need right next door to us.

Fireside Fellowship

"God, if You are there and You love me, You better turn my life around. I cannot take it any longer." The woman's voice held more desperation than defiance. As her clenched fist slowly fell back on the bed the sobs came again, great wrenching cries of despair that threatened to tear her small frame apart.

In the space of three months Liz Beck had lost her father, her mother, and her husband; and following a serious accident, her daughter's health was precarious. In going over her husband's financial records, Liz discovered he had borrowed heavily the past few years to keep his business going. There was nothing left.

Liz had grown up in a devout Methodist home in Athens, Georgia. Her family attended church every Sunday and never missed the Wednesday night prayer meeting. Those were happy times. But when she was about 15, Liz's active mind began to question what she was hearing in church every week.

"Daddy, I don't understand what you're telling me to believe," she announced one evening. "You take me to church where the preacher tells me there's going to be a resurrection day. Yet at every funeral I've ever attended, the pastor preaches them right into heaven. So who's going to be resurrected? And what's this eternal damnation where people burn forever and ever in a pit in hell somewhere?"

When her father had no answer, she became more and more disturbed. Eventually she went away to college at the University of Georgia. At the end of her first year she announced to her startled parents, "I've had it with these Methodist beliefs. It makes no sense to me. In fact, I have no use for religion at all. I'm through! I'm leaving college and going out in the world to do the things that are going to be enjoyable and that have meaning to me."

She moved to New York City, trained at the Fred Astaire Dance Studios, then moved back down south and opened up two studios on her own. She was 19 years old and making $200 a week, a goodly amount then. This was life! She had money, power, prestige, and excitement. She took up smoking, and though she didn't drink, she spent a lot of time with her new friends in night clubs.

Liz was living for herself, just as she had set out to do, but strangely, the meaning and joy that should have been hers was missing somehow. Sometimes a great emptiness grabbed at her as she looked into the degraded lives of the people around her.

The years passed. She married and had two baby girls. Though her life was full, a restlessness always nibbled at the edge of her consciousness. One day she gathered her little girls into her arms and lifted her face to heaven. "God, if You're there, there must be proof somewhere. What do I have to raise these children with? I don't have any convictions. I don't have any beliefs. Nothing has meaning for me. I haven't found it in money, prestige, power, or even in the church. And now here I am with these two children and my husband, and I have nothing to give them. If You're there, then help me find truth that I can believe in, that makes sense."

During the next two years Liz did a lot of searching. Then she and her husband bought a house across the street from some people who were Seventh-day Adventists. One day when her little daughter went over to visit the neighbors, they showed her on the calendar that the seventh day was not Sunday. This was news!

"We're going to church on the wrong day!" the little girl reported to her mother. As they began to study Bible truths, a meaning and purpose came into Liz's life that she had never known before. She found the answers she had been searching for all those years. Before long, she was baptized and in great excitement went home to share her good news with her father, who was now in his 70s.

"You see, Daddy, we don't go up into heaven and float on some cloud somewhere!" she exclaimed.

When her father and mother joined her in her new faith, it was as if the void in her life had been totally filled. She couldn't contain her happiness. If only she could give meaning to the lives of others who had felt the same hopelessness she had once felt! She could not be still! During the next several years she shared her good news with other relatives and friends until a total of eight had been baptized.

"I wish we could just open up our house and have it open seven days a week and bring people in here and love them and help them and be involved with them so they could know what we know!" she told her husband.

The Becks watched their daughters grow up, go away to college, and establish their own Christian homes. One married a pastor and the other married the president of Little Creek Academy. Life was good. God was good.

Then came the terrible tragedies that robbed her of her loved ones.

Liz lay like a broken reed across her bed, her mind numb. She felt that God had left her. But in this, her darkest hour, when appearances seemed so forbidding, He was working out His will, doing all things well in her behalf.

Two days later a lady walked into Liz's daughter's apartment, needing a ride to a place called Uchee Pines Institute. Liz hadn't been eating, she couldn't sleep, and was on the brink of giving up.

I need to get away, she thought to herself. *I'll just drive her there myself.*

She was so impressed with the program at Uchee Pines that she decided to stay. Members of the staff had Bible studies with her twice a day. They saw to it that she ate. And she was afraid they were going to walk her to death. But she did begin to feel better. Then in her third week there, a woman came in who seemed to be worse off than Liz was. As Liz became involved in helping her, she felt some of her own pain subsiding.

And she met someone else. She had caught the eye of an affluent doctor who was also a patient. He offered her everything—a home, companionship, financial security—if she

Liz lay like a broken reed across her bed, her mind numb. She felt that God had left her.

76

would marry him. He took her to Michigan to meet his family.

Her mind was in turmoil. Then a deep conviction began to grow in her mind. She didn't need marriage right now. What she needed was to sort out her feelings about God, to try and make sense of her life. She wanted to recapture the peace and joy she had once known that had given her life meaning and purpose. She needed to find God again.

A plan began to form in her mind. She turned down the good doctor's proposal and decided she would go back to school.

That's how she found herself back in college after a 30-year absence. She had no money, no job, and, by her own admission, "more nerve than brains" when she moved into the girls' dormitory at Andrews University in 1977. But she knew God was once again leading in her life.

Her days were filled with work in the bookstore, preparing for the class she was taking, and studying religion as she had never studied before. At night, girls began to find their way to her room to talk. And as they talked, Liz realized the need in their lives was just like hers.

They're trying to find themselves, too, she thought, *trying to establish their convictions and values, wondering if there really is a God, if anybody cares.* Liz understood perfectly. She had been there.

One day as she was walking on campus, she found herself in front of a large home. She remembered how, years before, she had wished she could have a house that would be open seven days a week for hurting people.

"Can't I have this place?" she prayed. "These students need it. Now. You could do this for me, Father."

That night she got a phone call from a doctor and his wife who were going to Pakistan. "We hear you're an older student in the dorm. Would you like to live in our house while we're gone?"

"You'd never want me to move into your house!" Liz laughed. "I want to turn it over to all the students at Andrews University, and there's no telling what shape it would be in by the time we got through."

"That sounds wonderful!" the doctor responded. "Come over and talk to us."

Liz moved in on Thanksgiving night, 1977. The following Sabbath afternoon she was sitting on the couch, praying. "God, if You want me to do this ministry for the students You're going to have to send them to me. I left the dorm in such a hurry nobody knows where I am."

That night after sundown the phone rang. Soon ten students were sitting on the floor while Liz told them about her dream.

"I'm afraid our church is so program oriented we sometimes forget we're to be people centered," she told them. "Sometimes we forget to stop and say 'You're important; I care about you; I'm listening to you.' "

From those nights of listening to students pour out their hearts to her in the dormitory, Liz knew that listening is an act of love, that one needn't be a psychiatrist and be able to answer all the problems in their lives—or even know all the intricate details of those problems.

"I want our house to be a place of warmth and acceptance, so that no matter who walks in the door they will feel they belong and are accepted just exactly as they are." Liz was warming to her topic. "I've been told that a smile can stop a suicide," she continued. "We don't have to have degrees to do that! We can start right where we are, no matter what our limitations, and can be that supportive help.

"People need people, and we need to be communicators with skin on. People are tired of hearing about what we should be and what we are not. We need to show it in our lives."

She even had a motto for this as-yet-unborn ministry: Some people will never know the love of God until they see it in another person. "Most of the time, people don't care what we believe. They're not interested in hearing the doctrines of the church. But they sure do know the way you treat them and the way you love them. You can unite with me and we can do this," Liz finished her challenge to her ten young friends.

They decided they would meet in Liz's basement every

. . . .

From those nights of listening to students pour out their hearts to her in the dormitory, Liz knew that listening is an act of love.

Sabbath afternoon at 3:00. Each week they would invite a different professor from the university to present a 20-minute talk on a wide variety of topics—creationism versus evolutionism, love outside of marriage, is there really a God?, broken homes-broken relationships, drugs, Ellen G. White, how to pray. Then the young people could discuss and interact with him, exchanging ideas.

"Bring your guitars," Liz invited. "We'll sit on the floor, we'll get acquainted, we'll break up into little groups. We'll share and we'll care and touch each other in a caring ministry in a way that's never been done before."

Like the first disciples, those 10 young people went back to their dorms and told their friends. That first Sabbath afternoon 35 young people gathered in Liz's basement.

Before long, more than 70 students were coming, packed in like sardines. Liz took a picture of them and sent it to the good doctor, the owner of the house. Alarmed, he sent a letter back. "There are too many people in my basement!" he said. So once more, Liz was house hunting.

The university people heard of her plight and offered her a large, two-story, faculty home. "It's right on campus near the dorms and church. You'd have to pay rent, but it's there and you can have it and have your meetings there if you want to," they invited. Liz knew the house. It was the very home she had stood in front of months before and asked God to make available to her.

She had absolutely no furniture, but it was just as well because more and more students kept coming. They sat shoulder to shoulder on the living room floor, spilling out into the hallways, up the stairs, even in the bathrooms, trying to listen to the speaker. And they were getting acquainted, sharing testimonies. One night 20 students had an all-night prayer session, praying for their families.

"I was absolutely appalled to hear what was coming from the hearts of those 20 young people," Liz remembers.

The students ran the program themselves, organizing committees to plan their different activities. There was the food committee, which arranged for the fruit and popcorn they had every

Liz knew the house. It was the very home she had stood in front of months before and asked God to make available to her.

week, the music committee, and the outreach committee.

They struck up a friendship with the young people of the Methodist church in a nearby town. The first time they went over to attend Sunday school and church with their new friends, they all camped the night before in the church basement.

When the pastor welcomed them to church the next day he said, "I must admit I was a little afraid for you to come in our midst some months ago because I was afraid you were coming down here to convert all of our young people. But we soon learned that you were coming down here to love us. And we welcome you."

One of those Methodist boys called Liz later. "Remember me? I'm one of the Methodist kids. Hey, look, I'd like to know. Could I move in with you? I'd like to study more about what Seventh-day Adventists believe." That's how he came to move into the mini-dorm she runs in her house, and how he came to join the Adventist Church.

Before long the students were practically pushing out the walls of the old house and didn't know what they were going to do. Some weeks as many as 160 students crowded into Liz's house.

Then Dr. Mervyn Maxwell called her. "Look, I bought a farm that has a four-acre field of brambles on it. I don't really know if there are any blackberries in there, it's all so overgrown. If your group would like to come clean it out, perhaps you could make some money to get yourselves a bigger meeting place."

So Liz and one of her young friends went to look the field over. Stretching out before them was a three-mile stretch of 12-foot-high blackberry brambles. It looked pretty awful. It was obvious nobody had done anything with them for years. The young man told Liz later, "I prayed, 'Lord, please don't let us take this thing over.' "

But that's exactly what Liz told him. She strapped a football helmet on his hapless head, ordered him onto a tractor, and sent him charging into those overgrown bushes to cut out rows. The Great Blackberry Bushwack was underway! As soon as he emerged, his face scratched and bleeding, she ordered in the rest of

> "Lord, please don't let her tell us we're going to take this thing over."

the troops, 120 strong, armed with pruning shears. (Thirty-five of those stalwarts were their friends from the Methodist church.)

At last they were ready to pick. Nobody knew if there would be any berries or not. But the deeper they went into the patch, the bigger they found the berries. Liz stood in the middle of the patch and cried.

They picked every day from 5:00 in the morning until 10:00 at night. Every morning they loaded the flats of blackberries into a little El Camino truck they'd borrowed from Liz's son-in-law and headed for the wholesale fruit market in Benton Harbor. In less than three weeks they had earned $1,300, a small fortune.

When they met to discuss what and how to build, someone suggested they remodel the large two-car garage next to the house, turning it into their fellowship hall. For $350 they bought an ancient barn, built in 1865. The boys thought it would be nice to panel their hall with this old barn wood.

The superintendent of their construction crew was a young man from the inner city of a nearby town. He had been deeply involved in drugs and alcohol when he had somehow heard of the Fireside Fellowship and stopped by one week to check it out. Attracted by the love and friendship he found there, he came back week after week.

For months the young people crawled around the barn, knocking down board after board to panel the walls. They hauled in the huge hand-hewn beams, bearing the hatchet marks of the original builder, to span across the garage. It took more than two years, working in between classes, building a little at a time, but they were having some tremendous experiences, laughing and crying together, sharing in many ways.

The group used the money from their second year's blackberry crop to buy bricks and build a huge fireplace that covered the entire back wall. When the fireplace was complete, the young man from the inner city crafted a beautiful plaque to hang in the place of honor. Burned deep into the wood was Liz's motto: "Some people will never know the love of God until they see it in another person."

> For months the young people crawled around the barn, knocking down board after board to panel the walls.

Their room was looking beautiful, but they were still sitting on the concrete floor. So with the proceeds from their third year's crop, Liz purchased thick, lush, wall-to-wall carpet and put pretty curtains at the windows.

Now their fellowship hall was complete.

The next spring Elder Maxwell called to report that the blackberries came on but were so tiny and shriveled they weren't worth picking. He had to plow them under. "It looks like the Lord gave you what you needed as long as you needed it," he said.

Every Christmas they decorated the rough-hewn beams with greenery and prepared special Christmas food. For some of the students who came, this was the only Christmas they had, and for some, it was their only home.

Liz did graduate from Andrews University, getting her degree in secondary education, but she's never been able to graduate from her ministry for her students. If she were to leave, who would be there to answer the calls for help that come in at all hours of the day and night? Who would notice the tense faces or hear the silent cries from heavy hearts? Who would take time to listen? And where else could she expect such reimbursement for her effort? Oh, not in money, but in lives affirmed and made joyful.

It's worth a fistful of paychecks to see a girl who once threatened suicide happily married and in her own medical practice. It's gratifying to hear the president of West Indies College say "The most happiness I experienced during my student days at Andrews University was Fireside Fellowship." And what price can you put on hearing a shy young man say "Everyone here is friendly to me"?

That's why this "gentle bomb," as one of her friends calls Liz, has kept her door open for her kids for the past 13 years. But even people as well "paid" as Liz need to eat. So she worked for and obtained a license to broker real estate. But her heart still longs to devote 24 hours a day to her "real" job. And her dream is expanding beyond the borders of the Andrews University campus.

"Wouldn't it be wonderful if there could be special houses like

"All those years ago when I sat on my bed after I had lost everything and asked God to somehow make my life count, I didn't dream that anything could have filled the void in my life like this ministry has."

this on every Adventist campus! Many of the kids have been raised in Adventist schools, but some have never read *Steps to Christ* or *The Desire of Ages*. They don't know the basics of the Christian faith. And there is so much pressure on them—social pressure, financial pressure, peer pressure, and academic pressure. They need a place to come to where they are loved and accepted just as they are."

Her voice trails away. She's remembering. "All those years ago when I sat on my bed after I had lost everything and asked God to somehow make my life count, I didn't dream that anything could have filled the void in my life like this ministry has. Do you know what these students have given me? How much they have changed my life? Over and over, I have seen God's providential leading in their lives in impossible situations.

"I have learned that there is no impossible situation! Just when we think, *This isn't changing,* or *This isn't the way I want it; where is God?* He is right beside us, working through the most intricate details of our lives. He does know the end from the beginning and has a thousand ways to accomplish His purpose that we know nothing about."

If you're ever in Berrien Springs, be sure to visit Liz's home. Stand in front of the fireplace the young people built and read the hand-carved motto: "Some people never know the love of God until they see it in another person."

For the hundreds of hurting young people who have come to the Fireside Fellowship, Liz Beck has been that person.

Upper
Room
Experience

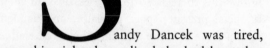andy Dancek was tired,
bone tired. Somehow, this night she realized she had been that
way for a long time. After putting in a ten-hour day as a literature
evangelist, she still faced a 125-mile drive home. Then tomorrow
she would have to turn around and do it all over again. She'd been
doing that, week after week, for the past year and a half.

There's got to be a better way, she thought wearily. Maybe it
would be smart to get an apartment or a room in her territory and
stay there during the week.

So she contacted area pastors and put notices in conference
newsletters. Nothing turned up. Maybe she should check the
newspaper.

* * * * *

Jan Hill dug her fingers into the sand, closing her eyes against
the Florida sunshine. She was so cold. Not on the outside—deep
inside, where no sun could reach.

In a few short weeks her world had tumbled around her. She
had been diagnosed as having multiple sclerosis (MS), her husband of less than two months had been jailed on his third DUI
(driving a vehicle while under the influence of alcohol) charge, and
her brother and a niece had died in a house fire. On the verge of
a nervous breakdown, she had to get away for a while and took
the train from her Virginia home to Florida.

Sitting up, she fumbled in her beach bag for the book she'd
been reading and found her place: "Every morning when you
wake up, you have a choice: to be happy, or not to be happy."

"OK, Dr. Peale," Jan said, snapping the book shut, "I choose
to be happy."

She caught the train back to Virginia, only to discover that her
husband, unable to cope with her illness, had abandoned her. She

thought she was going to die and lay on the couch, numb, unmoving.

There had been a time, years before, when Jan had considered herself a born-again Christian. It would be hard to say exactly when or why she fell away, or how she came to be an avowed atheist, defiant and proud, filling her life with drugs, alcohol, and worse.

Three days later she roused enough to turn on the television. The sounds of an Easter movie on the life of Christ filled the room. Too weak to change the channel, she decided to wait and see if something better would come on next.

The camera zoomed in for a close-up of Jesus' face. He was looking straight at her. "Don't be afraid," He said. "I will never leave you."

She sat up, electrified, her eyes never leaving the screen. "No," she whispered, "I don't believe You will." God had found His child. A certainty flooded her soul that no matter what, He would not let her go.

"I accepted Jesus that week," Jan says simply. "Within two weeks I went into sudden remission from MS that amazed even the neurologist."

She began putting her life back together, once more working at her job as an independent salesperson, selling eyeglass frames. And she began reading, hungrily, trying to learn everything at once.

Her large house, overlooking a peaceful pond, stood secluded among a stand of tall maple and oak trees. Comfortable, quiet—and lonely and expensive. Jan was not only lonely, she needed help with the rent.

One night she decided to pray for a Christian roommate. "OK, Jesus, I'm going to try You out. Send me a Christian lady." She paused, then added, "A salesperson, like me." She wanted someone who would understand her unconventional work schedule.

She placed an ad in the paper on Monday. Her phone rang on Wednesday. It was Sandy Dancek.

She sat up, electrified, her eyes never leaving the screen. . . . A certainty flooded her soul that no matter what, He would not let her go.

"Are you a Christian?" Jan asked abruptly.

"Yes."

"What kind of job do you have?"

"I'm a sales rep for Bible stories and other Christian books and literature."

"God sent you!" Jan hollered into the phone. "I prayed that God would send a female Christian sales rep to share my home, and He sent you!"

Sandy was floored, and not a little leery. However, she agreed to look at the apartment. But first she called her husband and asked what he thought she should do.

"Well," Ed replied logically, "you are female. You're a Christian and a sales rep. I'd say you pretty well fit the bill!"

So she went to see the house. "You will have the upstairs," Jan bubbled, still exclaiming over how the Lord had answered her prayer so exactly.

"I'll try it for a week," Sandy agreed, still doubtful. She stayed Monday, Tuesday, and Wednesday nights, then canvassed her way home on Thursday.

Every morning that week during her worship, Sandy prayed, as she usually did, that God would speak to her, letting her know what He would have her to do. Two days in a row she was led to Mark 14:15: "And he will shew you a large upper room furnished and prepared." She had to smile as she looked around her comfortably furnished "upper room." But the week went well, so she decided to extend the arrangement to a month.

Her days were long, and she would get in late. No matter. Jan would be up waiting, Bible in hand, wanting to know more.

"She had a zillion questions," Sandy laughs.

Jan told Sandy that she was an evolutionist and believed that she had come from the green slime that evolved out of the sea.

"*You* may have," Sandy answered, "but my heavenly Father made *me* in His image."

Jan was nearly speechless at that thought. "He did?"

"Yup."

"Are you sure? How do you know that?" Jan demanded.

"You are female. You're a Christian and a sales rep. I'd say you pretty well fit the bill!"

So Sandy dug into her stash of books and pulled out *Patriarchs and Prophets* and *Creation, Evolution, and Science.* "Check it out," she challenged, secretly thinking, *That'll keep her busy for a while!*

Jan read through both books, non-stop. By the time she finished, she knew she was God's created child. But the questions kept coming. Colporteurs work long hours. They get home late and are tired. Sandy confesses that some nights she tried to coast into the garage and tiptoe up the stairs. It never worked. Jan was always there, waiting. There was so much she simply *had* to know. How could anyone refuse such eagerness?

One day Jan suggested that they begin eating their meals together.

"That might be hard because I eat different food than you do," Sandy hesitated. She pulled volume one of *The Bible Story* out of her briefcase and opened it to the picture of the animals going into Noah's ark, and explained about unclean meats.

"OK," Jan said decisively, "no unclean meats in this house anymore."

At the end of the first month, Jan asked Sandy if she had made her decision to stay longer.

"I'm not sure yet. The cigarette smoke really bothers me. I'm not used to it and don't like the smell in my apartment."

Jan was immediately concerned. Then she thought of something else. "Do you think smoking aggravates my MS condition?"

"Yes, I'm sure it does," Sandy said.

"I don't want you to leave. I'll quit." She gathered up her cigarettes, broke them in half, and the two women flushed them down the toilet.

Jan had so many questions. Sandy didn't have the hours and hours it would take to answer them all, so she gave her three sets of Elder Charles Brooks' evangelistic tapes, along with *The Great Controversy* and *The Desire of Ages.* The questions multiplied, but so did the answers as the young woman drank it all in. Her excitement at all she was learning just had to be shared. She had been a Baptist once and just knew her pastor would be interested

. . . .

Jan was always there, waiting. There was so much she simply *had* to know.

87

in all she was learning. He certainly was! So she kept Preacher Charlie posted, blow by blow, because she thought he didn't know any of this.

After reading *From Sabbath to Sunday,* she was convinced that she needed to visit the Adventist church. She didn't want to and fought the idea hard for almost two weeks. Finally she looked in the Yellow Pages and called the pastor, Elder John Robbins. He came and studied with her in his gentle, patient way, taking time to explain everything to her. He'd never met anyone so excited about learning the Bible.

But war was brewing. Until a few weeks before, Jan's life had been in complete contrast to everything Christian, and the devil had no intention of letting her go.

One night several weeks later Elder Robbins planned to go over the baptismal vows with her, reviewing what they had studied. However, just before he arrived at her home for the study, Jan angrily ran out of the house and drove away.

Sandy and Elder Robbins knew the battle was on. God wanted her; Satan did not want to let go. They knelt by the couch, praying, asking God to bring her back, then they waited.

After a time Jan's car pulled into the driveway and she rather sheepishly came into the room. "Hello," she said in a subdued voice. "I'm glad you're here. Are we ready to study the Bible?"

Elder Robbins went over the doctrines, one by one. When he began explaining about the ordinance of humility, she became very agitated again.

"I'll never wash anyone's feet. I'll pass on that," she shouted, jumping up. She made a "time out" gesture with her hands. "That's it! Bible study's over. I have MS and my immune system is down," she ranted. "I don't know what kind of disease I'll get from washing the dirty feet of someone I don't even know!" She was terribly upset.

So was Sandy. Upset and exhausted. The events of the evening had left her drained, emotionally and physically. She didn't sleep much that night. When she got up the next morning, she still felt troubled as she sat on her couch reading *The Desire of Ages.* A

> "I'll never wash anyone's feet," she shouted, jumping up.

clatter on the stairs startled her. *Oh, no! she thought. What's going to happen now?*

Jan stepped into the room carrying a large silver salad bowl filled with water; a white kitchen towel lay over her arm. "I couldn't sleep last night," she said. "I have to make things right. God told me I had to have Communion. Can we?"

"Yes," Sandy said softly. "We can have Communion."

In that upper room this dear girl knelt at Sandy's feet and tenderly washed them.

Sandy had never conducted a Communion service before. "Lord, help me find the texts we need," she breathed. He did, and they finished their Communion celebration with two Wheat Thins and some grape juice from the refrigerator.

On October 27, 1990, five and one half months after Sandy first met her, Jan was baptized. This isn't the end of the story, though. In November Jan and Sandy got a new roommate. Who knows what will happen next!

Master
Teacher

Dr. Richard Orrison has been deeply committed to the education of Seventh-day Adventist young people for more than 36 years, the past 19 years as principal of Andrews Academy in Berrien Springs, Michigan. Under his leadership the academy was recognized in 1984 by the United States Department of Education as an exemplary private school in the United States.

Not the outcome you would expect from a college dropout who couldn't seem to find any academic major that "clicked."

After dropping out of school in 1953, Richard returned to his home town of Vienna, Virginia, and decided to find a job. Before long he was involved in the youth activities of his church, leading out in the junior Sabbath school and organizing the church's first Pathfinder club. In all this he was warmly supported by Mr. and Mrs. T. E. Banks, an older couple in the church. As Richard organized and worked with the young people, Mr. and Mrs. Banks were always associated with the activities in some way.

The Bankses had come to Vienna 10 years before to finish out the school term in the local church school, following the tragic death of the previous teachers. Richard had been in the fifth grade.

"He was not a trained teacher," Dr. Orrison remembers, "but he had taught very briefly as a young man and was what one would call a natural teacher."

A rather ordinary-looking man, slim and quite bald, Mr. Banks brought an ambiance to his classroom that was almost electric. He had some knowledge about everything and loved to take his students on "armchair journeys" to places neither he nor they had ever been.

Always there was music in his classroom, kids singing while he exuberantly accompanied them on the violin, mandolin, banjo, or ukulele. He knew all sorts of Latin phrases and had a vast repertoire of stories and songs to fit any situation, many from his experience in the Army during World War I. In his youth he had memorized extensively—poetry, prose, Scripture—and all these poured forth like a fountain when he was teaching.

When the Bankses left school at the end of the day, they always had a carload because about half the kids went home with them. For that matter, they had a carload when they came to school in the morning, too, because some parents left their kids off at the Bankses' home as early as 6:30. Once home, the kids swarmed with activity, making cookies, cutting wood, cleaning— everybody had a job.

"I'm sure they must have been bone weary inside," Dr. Orrison says now, "but they never gave any indication that they felt put upon. They were extended family to those kids."

On a warm August evening in 1954, two weeks before school was to start, Mr. Banks came over to see Richard. "Have you ever thought of being a teacher?" he asked.

Richard laughed. Teaching was the farthest thing from his mind, and certainly hadn't been one of the majors he'd explored in college.

"Well, you know you have the qualities that would make a good teacher," Mr. Banks continued. "We're going to need a teacher here at the church school this year. The board will be considering who to hire for that position in a few days. Would you mind if I presented your name?"

Richard was stunned. "Well, I guess that would be all right," he managed to stammer.

In a matter of hours after this conversation Richard had to leave on a trip that would take him out of town for a week. When he returned home, there was a pile of messages to call the school board chairman, Mr. Banks, and others.

"Lo, and behold, the board had voted for me to be the fifth- and sixth-grade teacher, and school was to begin in a week!" Dr. Orrison laughs.

On that first day of school Orrison knew he had found his

niche. "When I first started teaching, I knew very well I was using techniques in my teaching that Banks had used in the classroom when I was his student. For years I would think of him almost every day. He was such a prominent figure in my life that hardly a week goes by that something doesn't happen that causes me to think of him—an expression that was his, or some incident that transpired in our association."

Mr. Banks is an old man now, 96 years old. He's had cataract surgery, and though his hearing isn't as good as it used to be, his sense of humor is. When asked the secret of his long life he replied, "I crumble chocolate chip cookies on my cereal every morning!"

Dr. Orrison tells of a recent visit with him. "We talked of the old times, told stories, and laughed. As our visit ended, he said, 'Now I want to tell you what is most meaningful to me of all.' And he recited an entire chapter of Scripture. His mind is so full of wonderful things from the past that he doesn't have to feel alone and empty. He's good company for himself."

A life well-lived is its own reward, but it's more than that. Mr. Banks had an ability to inspire others to do good things, and as his life reached out to touch other lives, his ripple of influence broadened, extending to the thousands of young lives Dr. Orrison has touched and changed.

"Without question, Mr. Banks has been my mentor throughout life. He recognized a talent in me that I didn't even know I possessed."

Life comes full circle this year. One of Dr. Orrison's students is Kendra Banks, T. E. Banks' granddaughter.

. . . .

"His mind is so full of wonderful things from the past that he doesn't have to feel alone and empty. He's good company for himself."

Time Out for Mothers

Let's say you're mom to a couple toddlers. You're up to your elbows in diapers and can't find the living room floor for toys. You haven't sat at the table through an entire meal or enjoyed a night of uninterrupted sleep in living memory. *Sesame Street* is the closest thing to cultural enrichment that you've experienced in two years, and even though your audience couldn't be more appreciative, after your sixteenth rendition of "The Wheels of the Bus Go Round and Round" and the eighth reading of *The Bernstein Bears* you're fighting a strong compulsion to rush out in the street and engage the first adult you encounter in conversation—just to reassure yourself that you still have the ability.

Late at night, when you steal a last look at your dimpled darlings, fast asleep in their cribs, your mother's heart constricts with the aching love you have for them. There is so much more you want to do—you must do—besides changing their diapers and picking up their toys. But you are bone weary and, frankly, overwhelmed. You think, *There are support groups for people who have suffered bee stings and lost their luggage at airports. Why doesn't somebody do something wonderful for mothers of toddlers and other small humans?*

Somebody has! And, appropriately, her name is Angel. About three years ago Angel Bock started a mother's center program at the College View Seventh-day Adventist Church in Lincoln, Nebraska. She had heard of a similar program on Dr. James Dobson's *Focus on the Family* radio program and read Karen Spruill's short write-up about how she started a mothers' center. Taking whatever ideas she could find and mixing them with her own, Angel put together a schedule of programs she thought the mothers would enjoy and find helpful. She had it printed up and inserted in the church bulletin. From the pulpit one Sabbath she personally invited mothers and mothers-to-be of all ages to the first meeting, asking those who were not interested to share their schedule with a friend or neighbor.

Downstairs in the church Angel fixed up a children's room near where the mothers' program would be held, but not so close that the mothers would hear the children. She furnished it with a changing table and two baby swings she had bought at Goodwill Industries. Two sizes of disposable diapers, baby wipes, and Kleenex were tucked into the changing drawers. Someone donated a playpen and three or four boxes of toys. Each child's name would be written on masking tape and applied to his or her shirt and diaper bag. And most important of all, "volunteer grandmas" were enlisted to baby-sit.

Sixteen moms came to that first program, and attendance ranged between eight and 20 the first year. Now about 30 moms, a third of whom are not Adventists, meet in the fellowship hall of the church twice every month in a homey, relaxed atmosphere, conducive for sharing and visiting and laughing. The hour-and-a-half program begins at 10:00 a.m. with a devotional, followed by announcements and a sharing time before the guest speaker's presentation.

At one of their meetings Angel introduced the idea of having a brunch. This was such a big hit that the women voted to make it a regular feature. They voted to have it at the first meeting of the month, since everyone usually still has some money then and can better afford the $3 charge! However, no one is ever turned away for lack of funds. The church has budgeted a small fund to cover little extras like this.

At the second meeting of the month Angel serves free hot chocolate, herb teas, and juice. Sometimes one of the mothers brings muffins to go with the beverages.

Almost every program on the schedule is what the moms have asked for, with at least one program a year devoted to planning new programs and getting ideas of what the women want. Mrs. Bock has invited doctors, dentists, professors, and beauty consul-

Sixteen moms came to that first program, and attendance ranged between eight and 20 the first year.

tants to talk about parenting skills, better home management, how to build self-esteem, strengthen marriages, and make new friends.

The moms learn cardiac-pulmonary respiration (CPR) and what to expect physically and socially as their children grow from birth to school age. One time they shared home health tips with each other. Another time many moms brought their kid-tested recipes. They made copies, and everyone went home with a pile of new recipes.

During the summer months Mothers' Center activities include visits to the zoo, fire station, local children's museums, and picnics in the park with their kids.

They have a banquet once a year, and invite the dads or special friends, and enjoy a special speaker. The volunteer baby-sitters come too, and are honored with a corsage or small gift in recognition of all they do for the Mothers' Center throughout the year.

One of the most popular programs of the year is craft day. Interior decoration and craft store people demonstrate ideas for the home on a budget. For a small cost the women take home something quite nice that they have made. They've done such crafts as grapevine heart wreaths, Christmas candle wreaths, mop dolls, and large Christmas wall wreaths.

One of the mothers recently started a food co-op that she runs from her home. The bulk order the group places for vegetarian health foods results in substantial savings for everyone.

Members also have access to a lending library, which includes about 75 volumes by Christian authors on a variety of topics pertaining to marriage and child-rearing.

A new non-Adventist member brought information on how to start a baby-sitting co-op. This was implemented in January 1991. When a member baby-sits for another member, she earns points. When she needs a baby-sitter, points are taken from her "account."

Angel tries to visit every new mom in their church, giving her a darling bib made by some of the older women, and an invitation to join their group. She tucks a coupon into the Mothers' Center schedule that entitles the new mother to free brunch on her first visit.

News about the Mothers' Center is spreading. Five new members joined as a result of an article in the local newspaper, and many more called for information. Social services is now passing out Mothers' Center schedules with their Welcome Baby Program to new moms in Lincoln.

The College View church operates a Good Neighbor Center in Lincoln that provides food and clothing for 25 to 35 people every day. The mothers who come here are in desperate need of help and support in the most basic way. In January 1991 Angel started another Mothers' Center at the Good Neighbor Center just for these mothers. A lending library has also been established there, and counselors are available to offer information and support.

"The exciting thing about Mothers' Center is that not only are we saying we care about and nurture the families in our church, but it's a great way to witness to our community moms," Angel says. "I try to keep the program nondoctrinal but Christ-centered. I am very willing, however, to share my faith and doctrines, if someone so desires."

Mothers' Center nurtures quite a variety of moms, from teenage girls to women in their 40s having their first baby. Some have degrees, others are on welfare, all are welcome. Recently an older mom in their church invited a 16-year-old unmarried mom. At first she required a lot of acceptance from the other moms in the group, what with her wild hairdo, sloppy clothes, and ever-present can of Dr. Pepper. But she was such a little girl, they soon took her under their wings, sharing her pride in her baby daughter. She's been coming ever since. Recently she wanted to know about having her baby baptized.

"I explained how we dedicate our children when they are babies, and she wanted that," Angel says. Angel and her husband, a pastor at the College View church, had the privilege of doing that dedication service for her.

"Loneliness is the greatest stress of a stay-at-home mom,"

> At first she required a lot of acceptance from the other moms in the group, what with her wild hairdo, sloppy clothes, and ever-present can of Dr. Pepper.

Angel Bock concludes. "Every woman needs friends to talk and share with. She needs support from someone other than her husband, and many women do not have family support nearby. Feelings of inadequacy plague all mothers, especially full-time moms. It's overwhelming to know that the children are your responsibility to mold. That is why the College View Mothers' Center was formed. We understand a mother's feelings."

And with that understanding, the Mothers' Center is continuing the work Jesus began when He gathered the children of Judea in His arms on that long-ago day. The mothers were comforted and returned to their homes "encouraged to take up their burden with new cheerfulness, and to work hopefully for their children."

Walking
Miracle

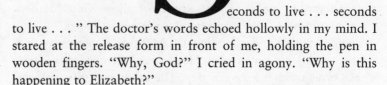econds to live . . . seconds to live . . . " The doctor's words echoed hollowly in my mind. I stared at the release form in front of me, holding the pen in wooden fingers. "Why, God?" I cried in agony. "Why is this happening to Elizabeth?"

We had been so happy when we learned that after five years of marriage, Elizabeth was pregnant. Things progressed normally until the seventh month, when she experienced sharp abdominal pains, then began hemorrhaging. Terrified, we rushed to the hospital.

Initial tests seemed to indicate that the placenta was abnormally implanted between the fetus and the internal cervical opening. If labor occurred, the baby probably would not survive.

Further tests showed the placenta to be positioned slightly to one side, and the doctors felt that a month of complete bed rest would allow the baby to grow, pushing the placenta out of the way.

A month later the hemorrhaging had stopped and Elizabeth was up and around. But not for long. Premature labor pains sent us rushing to the hospital once more. The doctors gave her medication to stop the contractions and sent her to bed again, this time for the rest of her pregnancy.

On September 1, 1988, after 13 hours of labor, she delivered a healthy 6-pound-11-ounce baby boy. We named him David Ivan Bermejo, thanking the Lord for this tiny miracle, and that the difficult pregnancy was over. We didn't know that our difficulties were only beginning.

Shortly after I brought Elizabeth and the baby home, my wife began to have terrible headaches that would not go away. I took her to the hospital where she began to have seizures. She underwent tests for two days, but the doctors were unable to make a diagnosis. They sent her home. The headaches continued for almost a week. On Sabbath afternoon she experienced more seizures, caused, we were to learn later, by a brain hemorrhage.

Once more we rushed to the hospital. Tubes were placed in Elizabeth's brain to relieve the hemorrhaging. I could do nothing but cry out to the Lord. And wait. That night the doctor told me that Elizabeth had only seconds to live. I needed to sign release papers, he said, authorizing him to use revival techniques should her heart stop.

Numb with grief, I turned to my family and the nearly 50 church members who had gathered at the hospital to give us encouragement and support. They began praying around the clock. I remember asking our pastor to anoint Elizabeth. Unable to anoint her on the forehead because of the many tubes on her head and face, he anointed her cheek.

Family, friends, and church members kept up their prayer vigil. Elizabeth's seconds of life stretched into long days and longer nights. Two weeks later the tubes were removed and she seemed to be getting better. She was moved to the Progressive Care Unit.

The next day she returned to Intensive Care. She had meningitis.

The tubes were put back in and a shunt was placed in her brain to do the work her brain was unable to do.

During the next two and a half months, Elizabeth continued to be moved in and out of Intensive Care as the doctors battled problems with her heart, lungs, and stomach.

The fear of losing my wife was overwhelming. At times I was so confused. Why were all these things happening to us? I prayed night and day, asking for God's peace, clinging to His promise in Philippians 4:6, 7 (NIV): "Do not be anxious about anything, but in everything, by prayer and petition, with thanksgiving, present your requests to God. And the peace of God, which transcends all understanding, will guard your hearts and your minds in Christ Jesus." And finally I could pray that His will be done.

I could do nothing but cry out to the Lord. And wait. That night the doctor told me that Elizabeth had only seconds to live.

99

On November 24, 1988, the woman who was not expected to live even seconds longer was discharged from the hospital. Elizabeth attended out-patient therapy sessions for almost a year and is now completely normal. She has no disorders or physical problems and has returned to work.

Sometimes when my little son runs to meet me and puts his baby arms around my neck, I wonder why things happened in our lives the way they did. I think about Elizabeth's nurse who decided to give her life to Christ. I feel the warm assurance in the core of my soul that there is a powerful, wonderful God in heaven Who personally loves and cares for my family.

And that's enough.

Miss Lovejoy's Legacy

I turned the volume up until the car windows rattled, allowing the rich harmonies to soak into the very middle of my bones. And yes, I was singing along at the top of my voice, in spite of the alarmed stares of passing motorists. Let them think another loony had been loosed on the freeway—it couldn't be helped; this music demanded participation.

The sound was unmistakable; the arrangements, unique. These were the Heritage Singers (plus me) in their latest album, "Commissioned," seven voices singing like an angel choir. After 20 years, they were only getting better, I decided. Definitely.

Since I had followed the Heritage Singers from their very beginnings, I felt that they were old friends, that I knew nearly everything about them. You can imagine my surprise when I learned that the real "founder" of the Heritage Singers was an unmarried school teacher in Eagle, Idaho, *not* Max and Lucy Mace, as I had supposed all these years.

Miss Lovejoy had not always been a schoolteacher. Before she found the Lord she used to play the piano for silent movies. And she was very good at it. She would thunder down the keys as the horses galloped across the screen, then sweeten the melody delicately when the hero swept the fair maiden away to a happy forever after.

Then, like I said, she found the Lord and became a teacher. The school in Eagle was housed in a side room built onto a little country church. Among her students that year was a fifth grader named Max Mace. The youngest of three brothers, he often sang with them for church and other special occasions.

Miss Lovejoy saw something in Max. "Max, God has given

you this talent in music," she'd tell him. "You've got to keep doing it."

She would stay after school, playing for him while he sang, encouraging him. They entered amateur hours at the Boise school, which was much larger than the little Eagle school, so Max could gain confidence in front of people. She taught him old ballads she knew and worked with him on songs he would hear.

"She just stuck with me," Max says now, "encouraging me. She never got bored and quit."

After Max finished the eighth grade in Eagle, he enrolled at Gem State Academy in Caldwell, Idaho. Before long he had formed a quartet. During the next four years the quartet sang not only for school programs but also for various special occasions around the Boise valley. It even made several appearances on television.

In his senior year Max formed a special student choir that created a little friction when it turned out to be better than the regular school choir.

Graduating in 1956, he moved to College Place, Washington, and got a summer job at the college bakery. That meant getting up very early. Max is not an early riser, but he was there anyway, even if he wasn't fully awake. Then one day this girl walked by the bakery window and Max forgot all about being sleepy. His life—and hers—was about to change forever.

She walked by the bakery every day, and every day Max would mutter, "I've got to meet this girl!" Maybe he should station himself on the sidewalk so he could say hello when she passed. Finally he discovered a mutual friend who agreed to introduce him to Lucy Hatley.

What drew her to Max? "I wasn't drawn to him," Lucy says archly. "He was drawn to me!"

Lucy was a senior in academy and was going to be a schoolteacher "when she grew up." An English teacher. She'd known this ever since Miss Hudson had made English so much fun in fifth grade. Lucy laughs. "Trouble is, I never grew up!"

Lucy and Max were married two years later and Max

Then one day this girl walked by the bakery window and Max forgot all about being sleepy.

continued his studies at Walla Walla College. He had decided to major in physical education and become a coach in sports. Though he wasn't big enough for professional sports, he had good abilities and knew how to figure out plays and find the talent to put together winning teams.

And there was music. Always the music. As he had in academy, he organized a quartet. Then a restlessness set in. Somehow he wanted to get out and make something happen. Maybe he would take up a trade. So the Maces—and the entire quartet—moved to Boise, Idaho. They decided to try to find jobs so they could keep the quartet going. And they did, for a year or so; but then the bass singer died, and each of the others went his own way.

Max took an apprenticeship to become a glazer, but after a year and a half knew that wasn't for him. Throughout the succession of odd jobs that followed, he continued to be active in sports, playing third base on a softball fast pitch team. They won the state tournament two years in a row.

In 1966 the Mace family, which now included two children, Greg and Val, moved to Portland, Oregon, where Max accepted a job planning recreation and activities for the employees of a medical lab. It was at this time he organized the Rose City Singers. For the next four years they traveled across North America in an old Greyhound bus, visiting Baylor University and every Seventh-day Adventist college, recruiting young people with degrees in chemistry and biology to come work at the medical lab.

It would be hard to say exactly when Max's desire to go into music full-time deepened into resolve, but in 1971 he got together with Jerry Leiske from Canada, who had a group called the Wayside Singers. They chose who they felt were the best singers from both groups and formed the Heritage Singers.

Armed with letters of recommendation from Jerry Brass, who was then youth director for North Pacific Union, and a supply of four-color posters a Methodist man had printed up free of charge, the new singing group (plus five children) loaded into Old Blue, a retired Greyhound bus they'd bought for $7,000.

Lucy remembers that day. "Everybody was staying at our house, and here I am trying to pack everything we own—to take with us, to be given away, or to be put in storage. I remember taking the last box of stuff and putting it on the truck, then picking up our suitcases and walking onto the bus. As I sat down and looked out the window I thought to myself, *Did we really do this?*

Those first years were tough sometimes, but never dull.

"It was scary knowing we had that many people to be responsible for. We had no idea how much money was going to come in, if the tapes and records would sell, or, for that matter, if anybody would come to the concerts. This busload of people were depending on us so that they could eat!"

Those first years were tough sometimes, but never dull. In addition to singing in the group, Lucy was responsible for the young people. Over the years, she's been mother to more than 200 kids. She's taught a lot of them how to sew on buttons and put in hems and do their laundry.

"It's amazing the things these kids don't know!" she laughs.

She helped Max with booking concerts, and she wrote all the letters. She worked behind the scenes, producing albums, doing layout design for posters and promotional material, producing TV shows, and, until the last couple years, making the wardrobes.

In the beginning they stayed in people's homes. They've slept on a mattress with just a blanket, and shared a bedroom with their hosts' baby, taking turns getting up to pat it back to sleep. Once they slept in a side room of the auditorium where the roof leaked so badly they had to get up in the middle of the night and put offering buckets around to catch the water.

"But the good far outweighed the bad," Lucy insists. "By staying in homes we made some wonderful friendships that we cherish to this day. I really wouldn't want to go back to it on an everyday basis, but I sure wouldn't trade the time we've spent out there. Otherwise, we wouldn't have met some of these wonderful people."

Perhaps the hardest time of all was the year Greg Mace, who

was in the seventh grade, stayed in Portland to go to school while his parents went on tour.

"We weren't making enough money to see him more than two times during the whole year." Lucy's voice still trembles at the memory. "It got to the point toward the end of that tour that if anybody mentioned his name I'd just start crying. It was really hard on me to have to see him walk down the runway leading to the plane, sobbing, and I'm standing there sobbing, pulling my heart out. That was the only sacrifice I feel we've had to make."

That's when Lucy told Max, "Either we have our kids with us, or we're going home. It's not worth it to me to have somebody else raise our family. That's not what the Lord gave them to us for."

So the kids accompanied their parents and took correspondence. In visiting 45 foreign countries they were able to see a lot of history firsthand. And Lucy got her wish to become a teacher, after all!

The group worked with a lot of evangelistic crusades, sometimes doing two crusades in one night. They'd sing at one place, then take down their gear and rush across town to set up and sing at another one. That was an exciting and rewarding time, watching families come night after night, seeing them take their stand for the Lord.

And there have been lighter moments. At one crusade in Walla Walla, the Heritage Singers were humming, standing in a semicircle behind Jerry Webb, the evangelist, as he offered the closing prayer. Just as Elder Webb said amen, Max sneezed, and his bow tie flew off and landed on the platform beside the evangelist. The whole audience got the giggles.

At a performance somewhere in Texas bats appeared out of the rafters and divebombed them. They've had "black beetlelike things" fly around their faces and into their hair while they were singing. They've watched mice run back and forth across the stage. And once a dog walked down the aisle, up on the stage, looked them over carefully, then turned around and went out.

"It's been a wonderful 20 years," Max sums up. "There have been obstacles; people didn't always agree with what we were trying to do, and we sometimes got discouraged. Then a young person would come up to me and say, 'Max, you're not going to quit, are you? I've grown up with you; you guys are an institution. You can't quit!' and I get the courage to keep going. Expenses make it a struggle to keep going. Really hard. But it's in the Lord's hands, whatever He wants. We've been here 20 years. If He wants more, we're willing. I know I wouldn't trade a day of it!"

Lucy echoes his feelings. "I feel this is what the Lord has called Max to do. He has a real talent to share with people. When you can help someone get his life turned around, it makes it worthwhile. It's the Lord who is doing it, but He's using us.

"At times people come up and say, 'If it hadn't been for the Heritage Singers I wouldn't have made it.' We'll get a note in the offering that says 'I was going to commit suicide tonight, but someone invited me to come to your concert, and I'm really glad I came.' Experiences like these give us the extra energy to keep going when we're right at the end of our frazzled rope. The Lord knows when we need encouragement."

The talent Max chose to use for the Lord has made a difference in the lives of people all over the world and in the lives of the 200 young people who have sung with the Heritage Singers over the years. As ministers, nurses, doctors, and teachers, their ministry, and his, is continuing.

The farm boy from Eagle, Idaho, has "kept doing it." Miss Lovejoy would be proud.

Wings of Steel

El Capitan soars 3,000 feet straight up from the valley floor of Yosemite National Park. Proud and forbidding, its rounded dome catches the first morning light. More than 60 different climbing routes crawl over its vertical flanks, making this world's largest granite monolith a rock climber's mecca.

Some of the routes are easy, taking less than a day to climb. Others are desperately difficult, requiring climbers to live on the wall for weeks as they struggle to reach the summit.

On a certain day in May 1982 Richard Jensen and Mark Smith were not considering any of these routes. The two young men, both in their early 20s, had been friends for two years and had become a highly compatible climbing team. They had been climbing five days a week for the past four months, getting ready for El Capitan.

Leaning against the mountain's granite toes, the two men studied their bold, ambitious plan: to establish a new route, a "first ascent," on the smooth, featureless section of rock known as The Great Slab.

Situated on the southwest side of El Cap, The Great Slab had repelled every previous attempt, primarily because of the horrible hooking conditions and the prospect of having to spend a month trying to negotiate the vertical blankness. The two young men had gathered food, water, and thousands of dollars' worth of gear—enough to last for 30 days on the rock. Though they prepared for every contingency, they figured the route they mapped out would take far less than 30 days.

The error of this assumption became apparent the first ten feet of the climb.

Their first task was to establish two rope lengths of 145 feet each. Once these were in place, they would leave the ground for good.

Right from the ground, the climb was fiercely difficult. They experienced a 30 percent hook failure. The sharp hooks, shaped like gigantic, heavy-duty fish hooks, were placed by hand into small lips of rock that sometimes were no thicker than a nickel, but the ledge must be horizontal or the hook would not hold. Half-inch webbing threaded through the eyelet of the hook supported the body weight. On average one hook out of three failed under their body weight, resulting in falls of various distances before the rope and other equipment would arrest them. By the time the first rope length was established, they had taken a combined total of 120 feet in falls, most of which were distances of 25 feet or less.

Mark earned the "distinction" of taking the longest fall on the route: a 45-foot, upside-down, back-to-the-wall plunge that almost resulted in his leaving his head behind on a small ledge. This same ledge had been responsible for Richard's dislocated ankle the day before.

Then a storm moved in, forcing the men back to the valley floor, to the shelter of their tent. As they soberly took stock of their war wounds, they began to reassess the magnitude of their undertaking. Perhaps this slab *was* unclimbable.

The second rope length brought even greater horrors than had the first. Because he had an injured ankle, Richard belayed the rope while Mark took the lead up the slab's 80-degree—almost vertical—face. Mark's first two attempts to climb above their first anchor resulted in two 25-foot falls. Each impact launched Richard six feet out of his belaying hammock and onto the anchor bolts.

The men were badly shaken. They lay against the granite, gasping. The knowledge that at any moment one, or both, of them could be badly injured, or worse, cast its sinister shadow through their minds, nibbling at the edges of their confidence. Later Mark would admit he was close to quitting at this point but was determined not to be overcome. After his two brutal falls against

· · · · · · · · · · · · · · · · · ·

The men were badly

shaken. They lay

against the granite,

gasping.

the bolts, Richard wasn't so sure he wanted that kind of determination.

Eventually, in one of the most desperate leads of his life, Mark managed to climb 140 feet past their first anchor to establish the second anchor. Now that the two rope lengths were attached to the granite face of the slab, they could haul up all their supplies, after which they would live on the wall.

It required a week of backbreaking, mulelike labor to bring their 1,200 pounds of supplies to the base of their route. The supplies were then packed into seven haul bags that the men hauled up to the second anchor. That job completed, the men left the ground for good on June 5 and settled in for their first night of living in a vertical realm.

During the next three weeks the climbers pushed their route higher and higher up the face of The Great Slab. The hook failure ratio improved somewhat, but they were still taking many falls for each rope length achieved. It became a classic example of "two steps forward, one step back."

Both men looked forward to each Sabbath with eager anticipation. It was a day when they could relax, read, and listen to music. But most of all, it was a day to enjoy the view. And what a view it was! They could see the "climber watchers" far below in El Cap Meadows, who spent their vacation days peering through telescopes at the climbers on El Capitan.

Peregrine falcons, nesting on El Cap, flew by almost within arm's reach.

The first time the climbers heard a falcon stooping (plummeting down the face of the wall after prey), their hearts nearly stopped because it sounded just like a rock falling, a climber's worst nightmare.

The falcon hurtled past them, wings folded tightly against its body. Below, a swallow, sensing his mortal danger, began a dive of his own, trying desperately to drop faster than the falcon. The birds fell nearly 2,000 feet, almost to the treetops. The swallow tried to pull out at the last moment, but was unable to maneuver quickly enough, and the falcon had him in a flash.

They were still taking many falls for each rope length achieved. It became a classic example of "two steps forward, one step back."

109

They were about halfway up the face on the twenty-fourth night when a major storm moved in. At first the rain fell in drowning sheets. Soon a deeper, heavier rumbling of water began to pound on the rain flies of their porta ledges, the hanging army cotlike beds they slept in. The rain flies, supported with a square aluminum frame, formed a pyramid-shaped tent around their porta ledges. While better than a hammock, the porta ledges were uncomfortable and confining, scarcely larger than their bodies.

"The water would pound on me for a while," Richard recalls, "then it would stop and I could hear it pounding on Mark. Then it started in on me again. We couldn't sleep and began yelling back and forth, trying to understand what was happening."

Slowly the awful realization settled in: they had unwittingly pitched their bivouac in a spot where runoff rains produced a crashing waterfall; it threatened to sweep them off the wall! Then the lightning strikes moved in. For three days and three nights the storm raged while the men huddled miserably behind their rain flies.

When the storm finally subsided, they peered out from under their rain flies, almost afraid to move for fear the "storm gods" would notice they were alive and unleash the cataclysm all over again.

They had survived what was later declared to be the worst storm on record in Yosemite Valley in the month of July. More than a foot of snow had fallen on the summit. Of the five climbing teams that were on El Cap at the start of this storm, three had to be rescued.

The men renewed their climb the next morning with the realization that they had now tied the world's record for the longest time anyone had lived continuously on a rock wall while climbing it. The previous record of 28 days had been set in 1972 by Warren Harding and Dean Caldwell on El Cap's The Wall of the Early Morning Light.

Twenty-eight days, and they were only halfway up the wall, seriously behind schedule. Food supplies were very low. They'd been rationing for more than a week. They were almost out of

Food supplies were very low. They'd been rationing for more than a week.

certain kinds of equipment they were sure to need higher up. It was time to take stock. They were about to head into 500 feet of overhanging rock from which it would be hard, or impossible, to retreat.

And there was one more serious consideration. Both men were truly sick of this climb. They felt beaten back by the unrelenting difficulties they had encountered, the frequent and jarring falls, the constant fear of dropping something or having something drop onto them.

Then there was the boredom of long belaying sessions, relieved only by the horror of leading, with its constant risk of falling and being hurt. Lack of warm meals and showers and no company besides each other had also taken its toll. Even though Richard and Mark got along exceptionally well, they were growing weary of each other.

Before leaving the ground they had made a vow that neither of them would bring up the subject of quitting. Their logic was that if neither of them broached the subject, then they could never quit. They began talking, comparing notes about their sad situation. And then, neither is quite sure how, they were openly discussing quitting.

Both agreed they really wanted off this climb, but in the end they just couldn't bring themselves to quit after all the time, money, effort, and pain they had invested. So with new determination, they headed up into the overhangs. They would make the summit. Or die trying.

To make their food supplies stretch, they would need to ration even more stringently, consuming only 600 calories per day. (They would each lose 20 pounds.) They took more falls, ran out of certain equipment, and had to improvise.

Finally they found themselves directly beneath a wide, overhanging slot filled with masses of green slime and white slime worms. Inch by tedious inch, they worked their way out and over this final hurdle.

After 39 days and nights, they staggered onto the summit dome, on rubbery legs that hadn't walked for more than five weeks. It was done. The new route, which they would name Wings of Steel, had been established.

Too weary to celebrate, they sank to the ground under a pine tree. Days of rationing had left them gaunt and hungry. They had nothing left to eat and it was an eight-and-a-half-mile hike to the bottom. Just as they were debating whether or not they could physically do it, two tourists came over the summit dome carrying packs that read "FOOD" on the sides. The weary climbers traded some of their water for the tourists' food. Leaving all their gear behind, they headed for the valley floor.

Five other climbing teams have since attempted Wings of Steel. None have been successful.

Richard, who is a house manager in a group home for emotionally disturbed young people, and Mark, who teaches at Orangewood Academy, were talking recently about the compelling similarities between their historic climb and the Christian life.

"In both, there are difficulties to be endured, costs to be counted, commitments to be made," Richard says. "I'm very grateful that Jesus climbs with us every day, ensuring that we'll one day reach the summit. The view from the top will be worth it all!"

Direct Line to Heaven

L et the little children come to me, and do not hinder them, for the kingdom of heaven belongs to such as these."
—Matthew 19:14 (NIV)

Wonderful things happen when God's children, whatever their age, turn their faces to Him, and in the simplicity of their full confidence and trust that He will provide, present to Him their needs.

Here are the stories of two literature evangelists whom God used to answer direct prayers in direct—and wonderful—ways.

* * * * *

"Big Week" is always exciting—and usually hectic, with appointments filling every hour of the day as literature evangelists concentrate their efforts in a special way to reach as many homes as possible.

Lon Boothby finished one such appointment about 20 minutes early and decided to go next door, even though he had no request card from that home.

An elderly woman answered his knock and invited him in immediately. The room seemed to be wall-to-wall babies. There were babies in cribs and playpens, babies scooting around in walkers, and babies tugging on her dress.

"You see, I'm retired." She smiled at the obvious contradiction of her words to her surroundings. "Many families in my church have two working parents, so I've opened my home so they have a place to leave their little ones."

Mr. Boothby spread out his line of children's books for her to see.

"Oh, I have books with pictures like that!" she said excitedly,

113

going to the bookcase and pulling out *Bible Readings for the Home*. She had recognized the books as being from the same source by the quality of pictures.

After he had written up her order, Lon asked if they could pray together. When the amen was said, the little woman looked up into his face intently. "The Lord said you would be coming," she said. "I have been looking for something to use with the children, so I asked Him about it. He gave me a dream that someone would come to my door and would have an answer. You are the very man I saw in my dream!"

* * * * *

Every morning Neil Busby would take his young son and their dog for a walk around the park that was down the street from their home. Neil always brought along a golf club and ball, and at each corner of the park the three of them would pause while Neil whacked off a mighty drive. Boy and dog would carefully watch the ball's trajectory, then run after it in hot pursuit.

One April day Neil had several lead cards to follow up on, so after their walk he took his briefcase and headed for the first address. He had barely parked the car and retrieved his case from the back seat when the door of the house opened and a woman came out onto the porch.

"You wouldn't happen to have books in that case, would you?" she called out.

"As a matter of fact, I do!" Neil called back cheerfully, wondering if she was going to end this visit before it even began. "I'm here at the special request of Shirley Nova," he added in his most positive colporteur voice, holding up his lead card.

"Why, I'm Shirley! Say, do you have a black Scottish Terrier dog?"

Now it was Neil's turn to be surprised. "Yes."

"And do you have a small boy, about 7 years old?"

"Well, yes, I do," Neil stammered.

"Were you playing in the park this morning?" Hardly waiting for him to nod his head, she hurried on. "I had a dream about you. In my dream, I saw you playing golf in the park with your little

. . . .

He had barely parked the car and retrieved his case from the back seat when the door of the house opened and a woman came out onto the porch.

114

boy and dog. I recognize you from the dream. Come on in." She held the door wide, then bustled in behind him. "And let me have a look at that card."

She looked at the card carefully through her bifocals. "Why, I sent that card in five months ago! I'd forgotten all about it. In my dream I was told you would be bringing by some books that I was supposed to buy for my family." She patted a spot beside her on the sofa. "Now let me look at those books."

It's not often a literature evangelist is left speechless. Fortunately, he was still able to fill out the order!

The Underwear Lady of Wake County

....

Ever since Adam and Eve looked into the wrinkled little face of their firstborn child, parents have dared to dream great dreams for their children. But when Pat and Jerry Fritz brought their dark-eyed baby girl, Donna, home from the hospital 25 years ago, having her grow up to become known as "The Underwear Lady of Wake County" was not on their list along with doctor, lawyer, or oceanographer. Here's how it happened.

While she was a student at Columbia Union College in Maryland, Donna volunteered with Metro Ministries, an organization that involves students in various community outreach programs. She became the director of the Big Brother/Big Sister program; her brother John was the faculty sponsor.

Just before school started in 1985, the Metro Ministries people got together for a brainstorming session. They were hoping to find a project that would catch the attention of a somewhat apathetic student body.

Sherrie Morgan, the Soup Kitchen coordinator, mentioned that while many of the shelters for homeless people had a good inventory of donated used clothing, there was no underwear. One idea led to another, and before the meeting was over, the Underwear Drive was born.

Together with her brother and his wife, Dawn, Donna went into action.

"We wanted to make it just off-the-wall enough that college students would give," Donna says.

Drop boxes were set up at various locations about campus, each clearly marked with a large sign encouraging students to "Drop Your Drawers Here!" And they did. That is, they brought new underpants, T-shirts, thermal underwear, socks, hats, slips, bras, even pantyhose, and began filling up the boxes.

That first year about 700 pieces were collected. The next year, the students donated twice that many.

Then Donna graduated and accepted the position of director of communications for Family Services of Wake County, Inc., in North Carolina. She had scarcely endorsed her first paycheck when she proposed, a little shyly, her underwear-for-the-homeless idea to her colleagues at Family Services. She anticipated their response. ("They laughed.")

"People think about giving clothing, canned goods, even toys for tots. Why not furnish the residents of all the shelters with new underwear. It's something that's really needed," she explained.

The rest, as they say, is history. As coordinator of the annual underwear drive, Donna has seen the program catch on in her community. And as awareness of the program increases, so do the donations, nearly doubling every year. In 1989 2,700 pieces were collected, and more than 4,000 by mid-January 1991.

A number of area churches are enthusiastically involved in the project, as are civic organizations, the Chamber of Commerce, corporations, and individuals.

And that's how it came to pass that every year along about November, Donna becomes "The Underwear Lady of Wake County."

A small idea. Looking beyond the obvious need to provide that small necessity. It has Christ's touch.

. . . .

"People think about giving clothing, canned goods, even toys for tots. Why not furnish the residents of all the shelters with new underwear."

Bakers'
Half Dozen

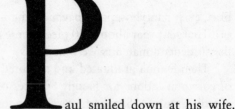

Paul smiled down at his wife. "Six down and *none* to go!" he whispered triumphantly.

Amelia twisted in her seat as the familiar strains of "Pomp and Circumstance" filled the auditorium. There he was—her last-born, marching proudly down the aisle to receive his college diploma! A sweet moment, this attainment of a dream that had been 28 years in the making. And somewhere along the way she had even managed to get a couple degrees herself.

She let her mind drift back over the years. She had been only 16 when she and Paul had married. Even then education had been important to her. She remembered promising herself that she would finish high school and have her bachelor's degree by the time she was 22. But what she had at 22 were no degrees and three children.

When she and Paul joined the Seventh-day Adventist Church, Amelia shifted her educational dreams to her children. Almost from the time they could talk she began asking them what they would like to be when they grew up. Of course, they changed their minds over the years, but selecting a goal became a natural part of growing up.

As they grew older, she began to ask them what college they wanted to attend. In their weekly family conferences both parents encouraged the children to voice their opinions and discuss decisions and solutions to problems.

One by one the children went off to school. Each year Paul and Amelia hoped they could send them to church school, but somehow it always seemed out of reach financially.

Then one Sabbath during an especially inspiring Pathfinder's Day program, the principal of Los Angeles Union Academy spoke about the importance of every child being in church school.

Conviction seized Amelia. For five years she had hoped and prayed, but now she felt an urgency she could not ignore. She began to fast and pray.

On Monday she called the academy principal. "Elder, your sermon impressed me. For years I've wanted my children to attend church school, but now I'm determined to do whatever is necessary to get them in. They simply must have a Christian education! Can you help us? I'm willing to work in whatever area I'm needed."

He promised to give her request serious thought and advised her to claim God's promise in Isaiah 54:13: "And all thy children shall be taught of the Lord; and great shall be the peace of thy children."

On Tuesday she found herself frequently reminding God that she believed His promise and was waiting for His answer. By Wednesday the principal had arranged for the three school-age children to be enrolled and had found her a part-time secretarial job at the academy.

Amelia was almost delirious with joy. That was the beginning. God lovingly opened door after door as He blessed the family's efforts through the years, sending one source of help after another.

During the elementary and academy years the children helped earn their tuition by selling magazines and working at the school. College was a different story. It was here that the really trying times began. Often they went from semester to semester, unsure of where the money would come from. But come it did. God always had a "ram in the thicket."

In this faith relationship the family established with God, they discovered that He not only supplied their needs, but quite often their wants as well. One summer the three oldest young people decided they would really like to go to West Indies College and Academy in Mandeville, Jamaica. Amelia agreed that it would be a good experience.

So they prayed that God would arrange it, believing that "whatever you ask for in prayer, believe that you have received it, and it will be yours" (Mark 11:24, RSV). Within a few weeks they

Often they went from semester to semester, unsure of where the money would come from.

119

had money, passports, visas, immunization shots—even pocket money.

The years flew by. The graduations began to come thick and fast. In 1971 the eldest son graduated from Oakwood College. A few years later the eldest daughter graduated from Loma Linda University and then from medical school. The second son finished at Oakwood College and went on to the seminary at Andrews University. The third son finished at Loma Linda, and their youngest daughter finished college and medical school.

And that brought them to this day when the last of the Baker children received his college degree.

Amelia sighed. God had been good. Very good indeed.

God's Will Ambassador

On May 24, 1990, Mayor Richard M. Daley, acting on behalf of the City of Chicago, inducted 25 "extraordinary Chicagoans over the age of 65 into the Department on Aging and Disability's 1990 Hall of Fame for their achievements and contributions to our city."

One of those extraordinary people was William J. Fillmore, age 75, the first Seventh-day Adventist and the first South African to be so honored. Among the many achievements he was recognized for that day was his 20 years of service at the Pacific Garden Mission. The mission is known for its substance abuse rehabilitation and for its ministry to the needy in providing food, clothing, and shelter.

From his earliest years Fillmore has devoted his life to a ministry that has spanned continents and touched lives from the ghetto to the throne.

Fillmore family tradition has always decreed there must be a William James Fillmore in each generation and that person must serve in the military. William remembers standing on the porch as a 5-year-old child, watching a man on crutches hobble up the front walk. When the little boy lifted his hand in salute and said, "Good morning, sir!" the man picked him up and kissed him. Home from World War I, father and son were meeting for the first time.

A generation later the scene would be repeated, only this time it was William coming home from World War II for a first-time meeting with his 3-year-old son.

William went to sea when he was 14 and married Daphne, the love of his life, when he was 19. For the next six years he was active in the Salvation Army and was responsible for the formation of the Torchbearers Group (an organization similar to Boy Scouts).

In 1939, when he was 25, he began what would be a tumultuous eight-year stint in the South African military, serving in Kenya, Ethiopia, and the Sudan. He had volunteered for medical work only, but one year later he was told he must carry a rifle and fight. When he refused, he was court martialed for the first of many times. His commanding officer intervened and angrily tore up his court martial papers saying, "A man of his caliber should never have been court martialed!"

William returned to duty. Before long he was in trouble again, this time for his opposition to apartheid. Military policy dictated that Black men received different medicine, medical treatment, and food rations than did White men. A White soldier was given priority medical attention, regardless of the extent of injuries of a Black man lying right beside him. When William treated all his patients the same, dispensing the same medicine and serving the same food to Black and White alike, he was charged with sedition and was court martialed again and sentenced to military prison.

William was already very ill with tropical diseases he had contracted while stationed in the Kenyan jungle. The conditions in the prison and the treatment he received there nearly killed him. Military doctors told him he would not live more than a year. He was sent home for further medical treatment and to await death.

At that time the German battleship *Grafstrey* was relentlessly bombing and sinking Allied ships along the African coast. The military, finding itself with a severe manpower shortage, dropped all charges against William, offering him the position of officer and an opportunity to live anywhere in the world. He declined the officer position, choosing to remain in the ranks, but agreed to go to Burma. Fortunately, hostilities ended before the transfer became effective.

No one was more surprised than William when, after eight years of military service, he received an "Exemplary Conduct Discharge" and, because he was found to be 95 percent disabled, given a lifetime pension.

Six months after entering the military, William became an Adventist. He had grown up with a familiarity with Adventists, as his childhood home was across the street from Sentinel Publishing Company (now the Southern Publishing Association), in Capetown. His grandmother often warned about those strange people who worshiped on the Jewish Sabbath. "Good people, but strange," she told her grandson.

When William was 14, a young Adventist man came to work in the shop where he was being trained in sign making. He and William used to discuss the Sabbath. William contended it was impossible to keep the day on a round world. Depending on which way one crossed the international date line, one would lose or gain a day.

Later, on a troop train headed for the front, William looked out the window and noticed a sign for Changamwe Adventist Mission. It stirred old memories of his Sabbath discussions with his fellow worker. Somehow he sensed that mission would play an important part in his life. One year later, back in Nairobi for vacation, he walked into the mission and announced that he'd like to study the Word of God regarding the Sabbath.

Years later, William would meet the very same young man from the sign shop, now a worker in the Adventist Church. He would show William the tree under which he had prayed three times a day for 14 years that William would accept the Sabbath truth. And William would be able to tell him that he already had.

During the next 19 years he would undergo 19 operations, including four major stomach operations. Once again he heard a doctor tell him he couldn't expect to live more than six months. Like Hezekiah of old, William turned his face to the wall and wept, asking the Lord why. He had served Him since he was a lad of 8. Later that night he was able to ask forgiveness and express a willingness to accept the Lord's will for his life.

The next morning he was so ill he had to be wheeled to the X-ray department. But one hour later he walked back to his ward on his own and was discharged from the hospital the next day.

"I cannot understand all this," his doctor said. "All the

> He had prayed three times a day for 14 years that William would accept the Sabbath truth.

specialists agreed that it was impossible for you to live more than six months.''

In the 23 years that followed his discharge from the military, he became the Pathfinder leader in South Africa, becoming one of the first individuals to be invested as a Pathfinder counselor in his country. He was responsible for the formation of 22 Pathfinder clubs, setting an example for his young charges by earning 45 proficiency badges in the process.

By 1967 he was in full-time ministry for his church, working as a self-supporting minister in South Africa, pastoring churches, serving on school boards, and holding executive committee positions on conference and union levels.

Some of the happiest days for William and Daphne were those they spent on the island of St. Helena, of Napoleon Bonaparte fame, situated in the South Atlantic Ocean. The Good Hope Conference asked the Fillmores to go to this lovely island of 5,000 persons to assume responsibility for the Voice of Prophecy School.

They soon discovered that other churches on the island carried heavy prejudices against the Seventh-day Adventist Church. Before long they found ways to break down the barriers.

They visited schools, prisons, and old-age homes, distributing Bibles and Gospel portions, and other religious literature sent to them from the British and Foreign Bible Society. Tapes from Faith for Today and Uncle Dan and Aunt Sue's *Story Hour* were given away. Each year Adventist churches from West Germany shipped them a large quantity of new clothing for the needy people on the island. The day came when the governor of the island came and worshiped in the Adventist church.

The island was a port of call for the ships of many nations. William made sure sailors from each of these ships received a supply of literature.

One day a large Korean fishing vessel that had been almost totally destroyed by fire at sea arrived at their island after drifting many days. The Adventists were able to outfit the crew with clothes. When William showed them a Bible, many of them shouted, "Me, me Christian!"

The Fillmores' comfortable nine-room home was located on the one main street of town, next door to the church. As the sailors strolled past their house, William gave them lemons, bananas, and apples from the hundreds of trees he and Daphne had planted.

When news that the Russian crew from the most modern oceanic research vessel in the world would be visiting, William prepared a poster with a Bible text in the Russian language on it. He set it on the sidewalk in front of their house. Then William took up his post by the front door to invite the sailors in for fruit drinks. The men were interested in the display of African artifacts displayed in the living room. They looked at the Russian books and Bibles on the table and listened to tapes of hymns sung in their own language. Each man left with a gift of fruit to take on board his ship.

The next day the sailors were back asking, "Please give us the Word of God. We are Christians, but please do not let anyone know what we asked for." Of course, William was happy to provide them with a large supply of Bibles, Scripture portions, and New Testaments.

On the Russians' last day on the island, they invited William and Daphne on board their ship. Since St. Helena Island had no harbor or landing stage capable of handling the ship, it was anchored a mile off shore. The couple was taken by small boat to the ship. An officer stood on each step of the gangway to greet them. Then they were taken to a large private area and served delicacies of cakes and fruits. Lifting high their glasses of fruit juice, this small group of dear Russian Christians proposed toast after toast to their new friends.

As William and Daphne were leaving, the Russians pressed gifts into their hands—hand-painted wooden eggs, colored postcards of ethnic groups in costume, match box covers, a picture of their ship, Russian coins and stamps. Then with tears in their eyes, they offered their final gift, a phonograph record.

"This record is of the bells of Russian churches that peal no more," they said. "But the day will come. Pray for us."

> The next day the sailors were back asking, "Please give us the Word of God. We are Christians, but please do not let anyone know what we asked for."

By whatever mysterious method it happened, word of the Christian couple on St. Helena Island spread, and months later William and Daphne would hear voices asking neighbors and people in the street if the minister who spoke Russian was still living in the big house. They would hasten out to let them in.

In 1970, when he was 56 years old, William and his family moved to the United States, where he became involved with the program at Pacific Garden Mission. In spite of his continuing illness, these were productive years for William. He completed four degrees, two of them after he was 65 years old (a Bachelor of General Studies in sociology and anthropology, and a master's in English and anthropology from Roosevelt University). He had to abandon work on a fifth degree because of weakness and illness.

In addition to his duties at Pacific Garden Mission, William became an associate pastor of the North Shore Seventh-day Adventist Church. He and a volunteer staff of 32 persons from the church—doctors, nurses, office workers, housewives, and business people—established The Way Out Inn, a self-supporting, non-profit project.

The group rented two large shops on the north side of town, using one of the shops as a kitchen and health food store/dining room, and the other as a book room where people could come in, relax, read, and spend time in study and prayer. Senior citizens could purchase food at cost value; others were charged a few cents extra to help meet overhead expenses. At times the staff gave the homeless free food and on cold days provided them a hot beverage.

Every Saturday night films were shown; other nights were set aside for games, health talks, and discussions. As many as 100 people crowded in for these presentations, including a number of young "hippie" women. They came dressed in Victorian attire, complete with old-fashioned brooches, necklaces, and rings. At times William had to "listen to their wacky poetry, but," he says with a smile, "they had to listen to mine, too!" They never asked for money; they only wanted someone to talk to, often opening their souls.

126

"I was greatly burdened at times," William says in his gentle English accent. "I would sense their need, and just there, in front of the others, I'd lift my voice to God for blessings and help. I only wish that I could have spent more time with those who came."

About this time the senior pastor of the North Shore church asked William to assist with persons who were depressed. He remembers one refined sister, "a lady in every sense of the word," who expressed a wish to die. Blind for 30 years, she lived alone in a nice home. Once or twice a week someone would pick her up to shop for food.

When William asked her why she had no desire to live, she replied, "Life is so empty. I have no one to talk to—no visitors, no real friends." Having lost all count of time, she would call William at all hours of the day and night with a request to "just say a word of prayer."

"Once or twice I became weary, sad to say, for there were others who phoned as well," William confesses.

Then one day she called again. "Brother Fillmore, I will no longer pester you. I have booked into a large old-age home and will be playing the piano for them." She had found her niche.

Those were happy, work-filled days. But William did not have a car, and he was often hospitalized as a result of plodding through ice and slush on Chicago's cold wintery days. Eventually he had to resign, reluctantly, as director and business manager of The Way Out Inn.

William Fillmore is a man who has always taken a personal interest in the world around him. Where others listen to the news and feel insulated and distanced by unfolding events, William and Daphne become involved. Since 1940 they have written personal letters to prominent persons—kings, queens, rulers, and presidents—whenever an unusual event regarding them took place.

"Without exception we have received answers," William says.

The Dalai Lama of Tibet answered their concern about the refugee problem. He included a photo and a book he'd written on the subject, both autographed.

> When William asked her why she had no desire to live, she replied, "Life is so empty. I have no one to talk to—no visitors, no real friends."

They heard from Mrs. Golda Meir, when she was prime minister of Israel, and from Emperor Haile Selassi, when he was restored to the throne after World War II. ("I was there when he rode into Addis Ababa on an ass," William says.)

At one time or another the Fillmores have heard from most members of Britain's royal family. In 1977 he was accorded an audience with Her Majesty Queen Elizabeth and invited to dine with her and her royal entourage.

Pope John Paul II sent them a Christmas card for four years after they wrote him a general letter about things of God.

And, of course, they've heard from United States presidents and their wives, including Nixon, Ford, Carter, and Reagan.

"A letter we especially appreciated was from Mrs. Pat Nixon at the time President Nixon resigned the presidency. She was in shock and very ill. She thanked us for our prayers."

During his illnesses William began to write poems. More than 15,000 of them. He received the coveted Silver Poet Award for 1986, and the Gold Poet Award for 1989. But that's not why he writes. It is his way of driving back the pain he lives with so much of the time, a way of expressing the profusion of thoughts that always tumble through his active mind.

Alighting from the bus one morning in late fall, William saw a man who had spent the night on a park bench. Here's how he describes it:

Stretched out full length upon a concrete slab—
    yet not a morgue—
A stunted log of oaken wood
    exposed to the cold of chilly night.
Overhead the stars keeping vigil, exceeding bright,
    pincushioned the heights of deepest night.
He greets new day with a wide yawn;
    with uplifted arms (adoration?) greets the morn.

They gather round, a curious throng—pigeons, squirrels—
    as out of his gunny sack

He scatters, he breaks the bread . . . transformed hard morsels . . .
    St. Francis has been born anew.
A Communion feast with bird and beast
    nature in praise, a benediction heard.
Indeed it is a rustic scene: the trees stand stark,
    scattered leaves of fall in gold.

In deep contemplation long I gaze . . .
    the golden shafts of sun highlights
The wide expanse of open park—beds of farewelling flowers
    breathe an adieu.
And yet, I sense things I cannot define—
    humanity, touched by the Divine—
"Birds have nests; the beasts holes . . ."
    this son of man nowhere to lay his head.

The fields and parks . . . hard earth his bed—
    whence comes his feed? Yet, daily fed.
All things are his, this pilgrim, wanderer.
    All around, the bustle of awakening—city, life—
Here alone is peace, pervading peace.
    Silence impregnates with sound;
The birds ascend to heaven's skies.
    Truly, God is here; we knew it not.

The Divine still dons the cloak of humanity
    as He walks the earth with men.

"The question I ask myself daily is: What have I done, what am I doing to make this world a better place?"

"I have seen both the heaven and the hell of this earth," William says. "A people in bondage, enslaved; poverty and starvation; unspeakable acts of brutality perpetrated against men, women, and children of all ages and color. Never have I lost my faith in God nor in humanity.

"The question I ask myself daily is: What have I done, what am I doing to make this world a better place?"

According to the mayor of Chicago, his church, and countless people he has touched through the years, he's done quite a bit.

Prayer Power

The halfway house in Washington, D.C., served as an intermediate stopping place for prisoners up for parole. The rationale was that a few months under the less-restricted atmosphere of the halfway house would enable them to adapt to the outside world more easily.

His work as a counselor at the halfway house often brought Eugene Toussaint into contact with these men. There were times when he learned firsthand and close up that some inmates definitely were not ready for parole.

One such occasion occurred one night as Eugene was making his rounds, checking rooms. As he walked down the long, quiet hall, hands suddenly grabbed him from behind and began to strangle him.

Eugene is a strong man—at one time he had been a Golden Glove boxing champion—but the surprise attack caught him off guard. As he felt his breath leaving his body, he cried out, "Jesus!"

Instantly the man released him, and he fell to the floor and crawled through the door at the end of the hall where he summoned help.

The next day he heard the prisoners laughing among themselves. "Hey, he was being strangled and he called on Jesus."

"Yes," he told them, "I did; there's power in that name."

Another day, as he filled out his report, a slight movement caused him to look up. What he saw made his heart almost stop. There stood a prisoner with a whiskey bottle in his upraised hand moving stealthily toward him. The two men locked eyes, and Eugene knew this man meant business. The man stood between Eugene and the door—there was no way out.

As he moved forward, brandishing the bottle, a voice shouted in Eugene's head. "Pray! Pray!" So he fell on his knees. And he didn't pray a silent prayer. He wanted the prisoner to know who he was talking to. When he had concluded his prayer he opened his eyes and looked up. The man was gone.

Several times during the night the prisoner returned to the doorway of Eugene's office, pointed his finger in anger, and shouted, "If you hadn't fallen on your knees I would have busted you up side the head with that bottle!"

Although he was certain the angel of the Lord had been with him, he was considerably relieved when the authorities returned this man to prison.

There is another incident of "prayer under pressure" that Eugene likes to remember. It happened one morning on his way to work. He boarded the bus and settled into a seat about a fourth of the way back. At the next stop a man carrying an ax handle got onto the bus. When he started swinging the handle everybody tried to push toward the back to get away from him.

As he came by, Eugene said quietly, "Mister, God doesn't want you frightening these people like this."

The man stopped, looking at Eugene incredulously. Cursing loudly, he promised to use the ax handle on Eugene's head if he said one more word.

As he turned to continue down the aisle, Eugene spoke again. "Mister, you must not have understood what I said. God doesn't want you frightening people like that."

The enraged man turned and once again Eugene heard the urgent command, "Pray, pray, pray!"

Slipping to his knees in the aisle of the bus, he prayed. When he finished, he saw the man getting off the bus, hands upraised, clutching the ax handle.

A woman rushed up to Eugene. "Mister," she cried, "did you see what happened while you were praying?"

He had to admit he hadn't because his eyes had been closed.

"That man raised the ax handle to hit you, and that's as far as he got. He couldn't bring it down!"

"For he will command his angels concerning you to guard you in all your ways." Psalms 91:11 (NIV).

The enraged man turned and once again Eugene heard the urgent command, "Pray, pray, pray!"

131

North to Alaska

Like a lot of other people, Marge and Arnold Ringering are retired. Unlike a lot of other people, they spent the winter of 1990 in Alaska. Since Alaska isn't widely known as a mecca for retired people, you may wonder what they were doing 30 miles north of the Arctic Circle. The truth is, they were working, making use of their recently-completed educations.

Until a few years' ago neither of them had more than a high school education. In fact, Arnold's education had stopped at the eighth grade. Then Marge decided to take nursing. Even with her family cheering her on, it was tough going. She became so discouraged in her final quarter she wanted to quit, but her kids wouldn't let her. Finally, when she was 52, Marge graduated and went into home health nursing.

She and Arnold decided they'd like to spend the winter of 1988 working in a rest home. So, leaving the cozy log home they'd built in Fairfield, Montana, they traveled to Arizona. Before long both became well known as gentle and compassionate caregivers. On the nights he was off duty many of the residents would call out, "Arnold! Arnold!" all night long. Arnold earned the name "Fast Feet" because he walks quickly when he's in a hurry—and a nurse's aide is almost always in a hurry.

The winter of 1989 found the Ringerings once again in Arizona working with their friends at the rest home. It was pleasant work, offering many opportunities to share Jesus with their fellow workers as well as with the residents. Perhaps they would have continued going to Arizona every winter had it not been for the trip they took that summer.

Marge's 80-year-old mother had wanted to go to Alaska for years, so they hooked up their travel trailer behind their big blue

Oldsmobile and headed north on the Alaska Highway for a three-month vacation.

While they enjoyed the spectacular scenery and the warmth of the people, they also became aware of the urgent need for geriatric nursing care. An idea began to grow in their minds.

The following spring, at age 70, Arnold received his nurse's aide certification and the couple decided to go north rather than south that winter. They chose Kotzebue, with a population of about 4,000 people (mostly Eskimos), located on a narrow peninsula off a larger peninsula. Vehicles, mostly three- and four-wheel all-terrain vehicles (ATVs), are brought over by barge to travel on gravel roads.

They arrived on August 16 and moved into an apartment; Marge reported for work the next day.

"We are in a three-story apartment building," Arnold reported to his children in a letter. "It has hot water baseboard heat. Also, we just got our winter clothes. We are warm."

Arnold applied for work as a certified nursing assistant, but was told there was no opening. The Administration for Eskimos is reluctant to hire nonnative help. So he found himself in the kitchen as a food service assistant.

"In three days I was working," Arnold wrote. "It reminded me of the Navy. I washed and set tables, helped prepare food, had scullery detail, and was swab jockey."

Five weeks later he happily took up a position as nursing assistant.

Although the Eskimos have been westernized in many ways, they still maintain much of their culture. Children are taught to respect their elders; they continue to feel responsible for them after they are admitted to the nursing home. They keep the large walk-in freezer full of meat—moose, caribou, ptarmigan, beluga ("white whales"), salmon, and seal (used for both its meat and oil).

One day a White man brought in a whole caribou, the first he had ever shot. Eskimo tradition decrees that the first caribou that one shoots is to be given away.

Arnold earned the name "Fast Feet" because he walks quickly when he's in a hurry—and a nurse's aide is almost always in a hurry.

When a polar bear is shot, it is skinned and the carcass is butchered. The liver, which is very poisonous, is released back into the sea. The Eskimos believe that in the future it will return again as another bear.

When the people of a village go out whale hunting and catch a whale, they pull it onto the ice, butcher it, and divide it among the families. The head is fleshed out and returned to the sea, not only because they believe it too will return as another whale, but as a thank offering for what the sea has supplied to them.

The Ringerings wondered if they would ever see the sun again, but their new friends assured them it would return—about the same time as spring does! Actually, it seems there are only two seasons in Kotzebue. Spring, summer, and fall are compressed into one very short season, and the rest of the year is winter.

There was plenty to do while they waited for spring. One of the hardest adjustments was their irregular schedule. Because of their rotating shifts, their bodies didn't know whether to sleep or eat. Marge enjoyed her work, even though it was many times heavy and stressful.

And there is much to be done outside of their work. They are actively involved with the little Adventist mission in Kotzebue, helping with the Community Services program that "sells" clothing. Eskimos don't like to accept charity, so a small price is charged.

Marge and Arnold don't know how long they'll continue in this ministry. Marge has been in frail health for years. She was born with a heart defect and suffered her first heart attack when she was only 42. She also has diverticulitus, so needs to be careful about that. She rarely complains about how poorly she's feeling, so one never knows if she's feeling well or not.

One Sabbath morning she woke up dizzy and nauseated with severe chest pains. She told Arnold she couldn't go to church and went back to bed. She really wondered what was going to happen to her; the pain was intense.

Arnold went out of the room and prayed for her. Then he came back in and said, "I prayed and thanked God for hearing my

> The Ringerings
>
> wondered if they would
>
> ever see the sun again.

134

prayer. Now I want to see you get up."

"I got out of bed," Marge says, "and I didn't feel dizzy. I felt weak, and my chest hurt like it has seldom hurt before. But I just stood there, and then I walked, because I wasn't dizzy anymore. As I walked, my chest quit hurting. I got ready and we went to church."

As she stood before the little group in church that morning and shared her experience, she looked at the upturned faces. How she loved them! How God loved them! She felt a great peace. She and Arnold were where they belonged. God would take care of their ministry in this remote place. And He would take care of them.

* * * * *

"There all who have wrought with unselfish spirit will behold the fruit of their labors. The outworking of every right principle and noble deed will be seen. Something of this we see here. But how little of the result of the world's noblest work is in this life manifest to the doer! How many toil unselfishly and unweariedly for those who pass beyond their reach and knowledge! Parents and teachers lie down in their last sleep, their lifework seeming to have been wrought in vain; they know not that their faithfulness has unsealed springs of blessing that can never cease to flow; only by faith they see the children they have trained become a benediction and an inspiration to their fellowmen, and the influence repeat itself a thousandfold. Many a worker sends out into the world messages of strength and hope and courage, words that carry blessing to hearts in every land; but of the results he, toiling in loneliness and obscurity, knows little. So gifts are bestowed, burdens are borne, labor is done. Men sow the seed from which, above their graves, others reap blessed harvests. They plant trees, that others may eat the fruit. They are content here to know that they have set in motion agencies for good. In the hereafter the action and reaction of all these will be seen" (*Education,* pp. 305, 306).

Many a worker sends out into the world messages of strength and hope and courage, words that carry blessing to hearts in every land.

Journey
Into
Light

Debra was a good worker, conscientious and dependable. She was in her mid-20s when she started working in the packing department of a large food company. When an opening was posted for a lab technician, she told the department manager she would like to move up.

She would need to pass a test, he told her, because the job involved mixing chemicals, preparing analyses, making computations, and filling out charts.

There was something about Debra, something he couldn't quite put his finger on. Seeing how eager she was for this opportunity, though, he offered to help her study. Time and again he went over the tests she'd have to conduct. She watched him with a fierce concentration, as though she were trying to burn his every move into her brain.

She was. Debra couldn't read. But in the five years she worked for him, the manager never knew that.

Debra's childhood was a nightmare of abuse and hatred and fear. Her earliest memory is of her father shouting, "You're so dumb, you don't know nuthin'." In time she came to believe it, and a door in her mind closed. Teachers passed her on from grade to grade, but nothing passed that door.

She used to dream that one day some kind person would come and adopt her and take her away from her family. This person would speak softly and dress her in bright, happy colors. She would be hugged and loved. She would go to school and learn and be a smart person.

Her voice is flat as she remembers. "You get pretty hungry to hear someone say a nice word."

She married the first boy who did, the need to be accepted and valued by someone was so great. The marriage was a terrible

136

mistake and didn't last long. Soon she married again. Her new husband had enlisted in the Air Force without telling her and there was no place for her to live. She had to move back home.

Debra didn't see her husband again until three weeks after their son was born. They were together for a couple months, but she sensed that something was terribly wrong. Then one awful night he tried to kill both her and their son. A friend helped her escape to another town.

One wintery night as she waited at a bus stop, a well-dressed man asked her the time. Not knowing how to tell time, she pretended to misunderstand his question by saying the bus would be along about 7:00. He paced around nervously, then asked her again.

She pointed to the bus just cresting the hill. "See? There it comes now!"

The next thing she knew, he had a knife to her ribs and was dragging her into a nearby alley. He raped her there, then raised the knife to stab her.

"Please!" she pleaded. "You can have my money."

As he rummaged through her purse a voice exploded in her mind: *Run!* Staggering to her feet, she ran into the street. His footsteps pounded on the pavement behind her, so close she could feel his awful presence surround her. A police car seemed to appear out of nowhere and the man turned and ran in another direction.

The police caught the man later, identifying him as the one responsible for a recent rash of rapes and murders. Debra was the only one of his victims to survive his attacks.

Then she got the job at the food factory and it looked like her life had finally taken a turn for the better. The dread that someone would find out she couldn't read sat in the pit of her stomach like a heavy rock. She watched as people demonstrated a procedure, knowing she'd have to catch it the first time because she couldn't read the manual.

Sometimes she would ask her girlfriend working next to her, "Do we mix this and this?" and get her to demonstrate it, or find

She used to dream that one day some kind person would come and adopt her and take her away from her family.

ways to get her to make calculations for her.

She'd been working in the lab for five years when she met Chris. He was unlike anyone she had ever known. There was a gentleness about him. They began to date. As they were watching television one evening, a preacher began talking about the seventh-day Sabbath.

"Did you hear that?" Chris exclaimed.

Digging out a Bible, they looked up the texts as the man preached. This was amazing! They'd have to do some more research. Chris looked through the phone book until he found a church with "seventh day" in its name. When they met with the pastor the next day he was most helpful, answering their questions, giving them books to study. And how they studied!

Suddenly Chris noticed he was doing all the reading. Pushing the Bible toward Debra he said, "Here, you read."

Fear constricted her heart. They had already set their wedding date. She knew that when he saw she couldn't read, the wedding would be called off. Hadn't she been abused in two previous marriages because she was "dumb"? She gripped the Bible, staring blindly at the pages. A long moment passed. When he realized that she couldn't read even a complete sentence, he helped her as she worked out each word, explaining the things she didn't understand.

The more patience he showed, the more she wanted to learn. Sometimes when he'd come home she'd be crying because she couldn't understand what she was trying so hard to read. Quietly he'd go over it, explaining until she understood.

"Please, God," she prayed when she was by herself, "I can't read Your Word. I want to know what it says. I know You can teach me to read."

The next week at work Chris talked to a friend about what he'd learned about the Sabbath. "I can't believe what I read!"

"Would you like to know more?" his friend responded. "I happen to belong to a church that observes the seventh-day Sabbath. Maybe you'd like to visit my church."

Chris and Debra not only visited, they were baptized two

She knew that when he saw she couldn't read, the wedding would be called off.

138

months later; then they walked down the aisle and were married in that church.

"We wanted to be together in our beliefs before we were married," Debra says, "so we were baptized together just before the wedding ceremony."

After hearing about a special program sponsored by the local library, Debra arranged for Mr. Leonard, a volunteer tutor, to come over twice a week and work with her. At 31 years of age, she was finally getting her chance to learn to read. Within seven months she had gone through four textbooks.

Though she still had some problems, she could now fill out an application. She could read what she was buying in the grocery store and knew what street she was on. It was an enormous relief.

But there was still something heavy inside. For almost three years it seemed that she was sick with one problem after another. Finally she asked her pastor to anoint her.

"Are you sick?" he asked.

"My past life constantly haunts me," she said. "I can't forget. . . . If only I could bring it to Jesus, like the woman who touched the hem of His robe, He would take away the haunting past."

And that's just what happened. "I don't go back into that distressful past." There's a joy in her voice. "I will always remember what has happened to me, but God has taken the burden away."

There's a quiet pause.

"Please," she almost whispers, "would you tell them in your book that my husband's name is Christopher Holland?"

H.M.S.
Robert E. Lee

By his own admission, Wayne Wesner never grew up, and there are thousands of kids who are so glad he didn't!

It's not that he doesn't try to "act his age."

"I just can't sit in a meeting with old people my own age and listen to them have no ideas, no plans for doing anything," he sighs. "I've always got to have some idea for doing something—especially with young people."

And such ideas as he's had! Working with juniors and earliteens in Sabbath school, Wayne was impressed by the awesome energy level these kids have, even when idling. Especially when idling. If he could only channel that energy into physical activity that was a learning experience and fun at the same time. There had to be a way. He decided to use his talents to work with the kids, helping them do things they wouldn't do otherwise.

Together they made soapbox derby cars and enjoyed Pathfinder activities. They swam in the ocean and took trips to the southern beaches to watch the elephant seals. Sometimes he took the kids to a small church somewhere and let them put on the Sabbath school program. He even conducted motorcycle riding classes and a couple seasons of hang gliding lessons. ("Without any injuries," he hurries to add.)

For 20 years there were weekend camping trips; then when Jim Crabtree, the new youth pastor, came to town the two men initiated the now-famous Rubican Back Pack Trip that lasted seven days and attracted kids from all over the country.

After they'd been doing the Rubican trip for three or four years, Wayne got to thinking. Their kids had developed into a gung-ho, strong, happy group who practically had it made in life already. They were going for it—knew what they wanted and how to get there. But there were other kids, the ones who were not physically fit enough to do a seven-day pack trip in the high Sierras. Why not do something they could participate in? So he talked to Pastor Jim.

"Let's build a raft," Wayne suggested. "Just a cheap one, and put a little outboard motor on it and take it up by Redding. We'll get a group of kids to go and spend a week or two, whatever it takes to float all the way to the Golden Gate."

"Hey!" his friend responded. "Great idea! What an adventure!"

The next day Wayne called Jim again. "You know that idea I was talking about yesterday? That's a dumb idea. You know who will go on a trip like that? The same kids who go backpacking. We need to do something that if a kid can do no more than hobble down the bank and fall onto the boat he can have an adventure on the river. What we need is a riverboat."

Jim was a little skeptical. But now that he had thought the thought, Wayne was off and running. "We don't have to make it too big." He began to doodle a little on paper and came up with a plan for a riverboat that would hold some 20 kids.

The two men presented their plan to the kids. If area business people would donate materials, and if the kids were willing to work with Jim and Wayne in supplying the labor, they would build a riverboat. The riverboat would be used to help other kids, especially in the promotion of a drug-free lifestyle. The young people adopted the plan enthusiastically.

Wayne held up a cautioning hand. "First, we want to know if the Lord is with us in this," he told them. "We'll visit three businessmen in town. If they say they'll donate materials for the boat, we'll go ahead with our plans. If three people turn us down, we'll go back to backpacking and forget this whole thing."

So Wayne got busy and made a model of the boat, put it under his arm, and headed downtown. His first stop was the Lumberjack Stores.

"We've been looking for some type of community service," the manager responded.

Three weeks later when Wayne met with him and the regional manager, they told him they would donate not only all the wood for the boat, but Wayne should give them a complete materials list as well. When Wayne saw their eagerness to help, he went right home and tore up his first plans and drew up a plan for a boat twice as big, and doubled the materials list.

Other contacts were made. Business and professional people around town donated money to buy steel and other items that weren't donated. They were on their way!

Wayne is a building contractor, not a boat designer, but he knew what he wanted. He'd seen a picture of a real riverboat on the Mississippi, the 100-year-old *Robert E. Lee*. They would make a sidewheeler like that great boat, big enough to comfortably take on a whole classroom of kids at one time. And they would name their boat the *Robert E. Lee* too, because General Lee was not only a brilliant soldier and considerate gentleman, he also had a noble character. He never smoked, drank alcohol, chewed tobacco, or took the Lord's name in vain. That fit well with the mission of their boat.

The months went by. Work on the boat moved along nicely. The main deck frame, weighing 2,500 pounds, was now welded together. The frame needed to be lifted onto six-foot pipe columns before the rest of the construction could be done. This way, when the boat was finished, they would back a semi-trailer underneath, lower the boat onto it, and move it to the river.

Wayne figured they'd have to rent a forklift or crane to move the frame onto the pegs. "If we only had a busload of Israelites such as the Egyptians used to build the pyramids, we could lift this frame into the air," he lamented.

"I think I know where one is!" Jim told him. "They're not Israelites, but there's a busload of students from Pacific Union College—the tumbling team. They're putting on a demonstration at Sacramento Adventist Academy."

Jim arranged for the bus driver to stop by the boat building site on his way back to PUC. And that's how 40 acrobats happened to turn up at the building site.

> When Wayne saw their eagerness to help, he went right home and tore up his first plans and drew up a plan for a boat twice as big.

"Here's what we're going to do," Wayne told the young people. "We want you to lift this frame up in the air and hold it while we bolt these legs onto the side of it. It'll just take a couple of minutes."

"Hey, we can't lift that over our heads. It weighs more than a Volkswagen," somebody objected.

"Forty of you can do it," Wayne assured them. "If nobody laughs!"

So they all pressed the frame over their heads. When the taller kids lifted, the shorter kids' feet came off the ground, leaving them dangling. But the job got done, and it wasn't necessary to rent a crane!

The boat was nearing completion. The pontoons were in place and the boat was painted and looking great. But they had no engine yet. Wayne had an outboard motor and one of the young people had another. They figured that the two motors would work if they couldn't get a diesel engine as they really wanted. Jim felt they should make the motor mounts and get the outboards hooked up. But Wayne held back.

"I think the Lord has a diesel for us somewhere but we just don't know where."

About that time Ken Giese stopped by to show his out-of-town brother the project. Ken had donated the use of his welder for making and attaching the pontoons. As they looked over the boat he asked where the engine was. Wayne told him they didn't have it yet, but explained what they were looking for.

"I think I know where you can get one," Ken's brother told him. "Mather Auto Dismantlers has some brand-new six-cylinder engines that have been imported by Mitsubishi for use in Dodge trucks. Something like that would be ideal for the boat!"

The very next day Wayne set off for Mather's and, sure enough, there sat a beautiful engine. Perfect, except for one thing: the $4,000 price tag.

"I want that engine," Wayne told the salesman. "You talk it over with whoever owns this place and see what the best price is you can offer me."

"I think the Lord has a diesel for us somewhere but we just don't know where."

"We're going to make the engine room to fit that engine," he told Jim. A week later, he went back and measured the engine and proceeded to build the engine room. He went to Mather's every week to get measurements. On each visit he'd ask, "What's the best price you can do for me this week?" and the price kept coming down, about $400 every week. This went on for almost a month, until the engine room was all ready.

Then Wayne gathered up some chocolate truffles, roses, and bottles of sparkling cider and paid a visit to a few people in the community who he knew were supportive of the boat project. Presenting his gifts, along with a little card describing their needs for a diesel engine, he made the rounds. Within a week the money began coming in.

When he had $500 in hand, he stopped by Jim's house. "Judy, Jim and I have prayed about this for a month, and now I want you to pray," he told Jim's wife. "I've got $500 and I want to make a deal today for the engine."

So the three of them—Wayne, Jim, and Judy—knelt down, and Judy prayed that Wayne would come home with a deal for a diesel. And off to Mather's Wayne went. "I'm having a hard time getting the money for that engine. I think you guys should make a donation toward this boat," he suggested to the owner.

They talked a bit, then the owner said, "The very best we can do is $1,700."

"Will you take $500 down and the balance in 30 days?" Wayne asked, barely able to conceal his excitement.

And so the deal was struck. By the next week the balance came in from Wayne's truffle/rose campaign and the engine was theirs.

At the boat's christening on Memorial Day weekend, 1989, a little more than two years after they began construction, Wayne met over 3,000 people at the open house held on the main dock in Old Sacramento where the *Robert E. Lee* was docked. Between June and December he hosted more than 400 youth and 200 adults on board.

The dream had come true! How many hours of labor had

gone into this dream? "We didn't keep track," Wayne laughs. "It was a lot of work, but working with the young people was a happy time. Lots of times they would come over and talk more than they would work. I might have to lean on them a little and maybe do some of the work over after they left. But just having them there participating was worth it."

The value of the materials and cash that went into the boat is $50,000—more material was donated than cash—but the boat is valued at $100,000. This beautiful riverboat, 60 feet long and 16 feet wide, with two decks, can accommodate 50 people at a time. Operating from spring to fall, its mission is to ply the waters of the Sacramento River from the northernmost navigable point down to Stockton and over to the Bay Area.

The boat is staffed by a crew of high school and college students who extol the virtues of a lifestyle free of chemical dependency and serve as role models for the kids who come aboard. During the cruise, the guests enjoy puppet shows, skits, videos, and personal counseling to teach good health habits.

Mainly, it's a happy time on board. The crew wants the children to associate the enjoyable time with the enjoyment and happiness they'll have with an abuse-free lifestyle.

The *Robert E. Lee* has been operating for two summers now. All kinds of community interaction has opened up to the young people because of their boat. Kids from all walks of life have come on board. The California Youth Authority, an agency that deals with youthful offenders, signs out groups of kids to Wayne and sends them down to the riverboat with guards, on Wayne's guarantee to bring them back. They often spend the weekend on board.

Small children who visit the boat are allowed to steer for a minute or so, kneeling on the captain's stool in order to see out. Then they get an honorary captain's certificate with a gold star that says they steered the boat without crashing and that they promise to steer their lives clear of drugs. They love it!

One of their good trips last summer was a "sightseeing" trip for the blind. Twenty-five blind people of all ages enjoyed a cruise

The boat is staffed by a crew of high school and college students who extol the virtues of a lifestyle free of chemical dependency.

up and down the river, while Wayne explained the sights and sounds along the way. A group of disabled teenagers enjoyed a tour of the waterfront. Helpers pushed their wheelchairs to the top deck where they had an unobstructed view of everything.

The boat runs trips for the Sacramento History Museum. They send fourth, fifth, and sixth graders on board for a two-hour early California history cruise. The kids enjoy lunch on board while learning a little river history and about the benefits of a drug-free life.

Last year the boat was in dock for the annual Children's Festival. The streets of Old Sacramento were blocked off while thousands of children played games in the streets, enjoyed face painting, native dances, ethnic programs, and foods—a wonderful time of kids coming together. Eight hundred families came on board that afternoon.

Next spring when the water is high, Wayne hopes to take the boat for 75 miles up the Sacramento, to every little town and village along the way, inviting school kids and townspeople aboard for an open house. Wayne's still dreaming. He'd like to have a great riverboat race in the summer, with all the commercial riverboats that ply the river. Most of the captains have tentatively agreed. Each would take on passengers for this race. (Actually, it would be more of a parade than a race. The river's not big enough for very many boats side by side.)

The riverboats would donate their time, and the people who ride would bid for seats. Of course, the *Robert E. Lee* would reserve its seats for children. People could send in contributions for youth charities in Sacramento—Heart to Heart, People Reaching Out, Big Brother/Big Sister, Boy Scouts, and Girl Scouts. Wayne thinks this race could become a major fund-raiser, bringing in $1 million for these community charities.

This unusual project for the youth of the Sacramento Valley began as a dream with Wayne Wesner in 1987. Two years later, with the help of volunteer youth and the encouragement and support of local sponsors, this dream became a reality that has

Next spring when the water is high, Wayne hopes to take the boat for 75 miles up the Sacramento.

blessed not only the Adventist young people, but an entire community as well.

One person can make a difference in this world. And Wayne Wesner certainly has!

Paid
in Full

In a world of corrupt television preachers and of government bailouts of shady savings and loans corporations, Gram is an anomaly. In a time when life is no longer simple, when a person has to hedge his bets and assess the situation, cutting corners here and there if he expects to survive, Gram's black-and-white honesty comes across as, well, naive. And as long as we're talking about it, we might as well mention that she's also stubborn.

Psychologists would say Gram is the way she is because of both heredity and environment. Gram would say she doesn't care what psychologists say.

She was one of 13 children born to Norwegian immigrants at the turn of the century, a quiet child who watched more than she talked. Her father had staked a claim on a homestead in eastern Montana. The land, like an old man turned stingy from years of frugal living, yielded up its meager crops of alfalfa grudgingly. Long days of hard toil provided not much more than marginal survival for his large family.

Small rural schools that operated six months of the year provided the only education available to the settlers' children. Not too many finished the eighth grade. But Gram did. It was her only window to a world outside the desolate prairie of her existence.

When she was 17 she left home for the first time to become the hired girl for a wealthy family. That's where she learned there was such a thing as high school, and she wanted to go.

It would mean studying far into the night after the housework was done. It would mean feeling different from the other students because she had only two changes of clothes and no time to take part in school activities. But getting an education would also mean that she would move from looking out the window at the world to walking through the door. She enrolled and graduated three and a half years later as a teacher.

She taught for several years near her home on the Musselshell River before she met and married Art. Their first child was born on a cold January morning two years later. Their second baby was born in December of that same year.

By the time the third baby came the following year, the country was in the grip of the Great Depression and work was hard to get. While Art picked up work wherever he could find it, Gram went back to teaching school. She asked the doctor to induce labor during Christmas break because she would need to be back in the classroom in January. And she was, often walking the mile from home to the small school in hip-deep snow.

The next seven years saw the birth of six more children, including tiny twin daughters, born prematurely, who did not survive. Shortly before the birth of their last child, the couple joined the little Adventist church in Darby, Montana. Suddenly their life had purpose and focus. Eagerly they studied, trying to absorb everything at once.

Four years later, Art became a colporteur. By this time several of the children were enrolled in church school, and others in academy. It was tough going. There were school bills to pay—and a sizable amount due the Montana Conference for Art's inventory of colporteur books. Regretfully, he left the colporteur work and Gram went back to teaching.

Six years later, Art was killed in a logging accident. He had been in business for himself less than a year. Adding to the trauma of his death was the fact that he owed thousands of dollars. Equipment was sold and the proceeds were divided among the various creditors, but there wasn't enough to pay anyone in full. Even so, the probate judge said Art's accounts were considered settled.

The judge may have considered them settled, but not Gram. She had copies of every bill and she vowed she'd pay them all.

She continued to teach, going to school in the summers to work on her college degree. She had been planning and saving to send her youngest to college. It looked like it was going to happen. Then she had emergency gall bladder surgery. In the process of the surgery, the doctor discovered cancer throughout her entire small intestine.

The doctor, a devout Mormon Christian, met with Gram's family. "It doesn't look good," he told them honestly. "But your mother has a strong faith; we don't want to set time limits that would get in the way of whatever God wants to do for her."

"I've got a daughter to get through college. What do I need to do?" Gram asked the doctor.

What she needed to do was submit to massive doses of radiation twice a week, which left her nauseated and weak. "And we have no assurance that any of this will do any good," the doctor warned her children.

She finished the treatments and signed a contract to teach school in Moab, Utah. Withdrawing the last money from her checking account, she purchased a one-way train ticket to Andrews University and told her daughter to pack her trunk.

Years later she was in for a physical check-up. As the doctor reviewed her medical history he asked the usual questions about heart trouble and diabetes. "Anything else?" he asked, looking up.

"I had cancer once," she said quietly.

Forty years after graduating from high school, she got her B.A. in Elementary Education and retired. She got out the brown accordion file where she kept the now-yellowing old bills. Over the next 20 years she began to pay them off, one at a time, from her Social Security pension.

"But, Gram," her children protested, "those bills are so old the people are probably dead by now!"

She set her jaw. "Then I'll send the money to their kids!"

She paid the doctor who had delivered two of her babies 55 years before. (He was now 94 years old.) She paid the woman who had stayed with the children while she was in the hospital having babies number four and five. (Each hospital stay was a two-week stint in those days.) The man who drove the logging truck for Art had never received his last month's wages, and a long-ago

She got out the brown accordion file where she kept the now-yellowing old bills.

150

landlord had two months' rent coming. There was money owed for groceries consumed 33 years before. Gram tracked them down and paid them all.

Now there was only one bill left—the more than $2,400 owed the Montana Conference. She decided she would save until she had the full amount. Month after month, she put money away. It took her nearly two years, but 39 years after the debt was incurred, it was paid off.

In her words, Gram was now "square with the world." The truth is, there was never a time in her 88 years when she hadn't been.

The Second
Mile

The manuscript for this book was nearly finished when I asked Gail Kapusta, my friend and coworker, if she would give it a critical read-through. She honestly tried, but she became so caught up in your stories, in how the Lord is using you to make a difference, that she forgot about being critical. Instead, she found herself praying, "Lord, why don't experiences like these happen to me? Why can't You use me like You use Claudie and the Clown Lady and the Keiths with their college kids? I want an experience, too!"

Have you noticed how the Lord is quick to pick up on prayers like that? Two days later Gail, her husband, Tom, and their son Matthew got into their car to begin the long trip to Florida to spend Christmas with her parents. As usual, they bowed their heads and asked for travel mercies. "And," Gail reminded the Lord, "send someone across our path for us to minister to."

On the way out of town Tom stopped at an automatic teller machine to get their travel cash. Gail watched him step into the pre-dawn darkness and let himself into the dimly-lit building.

"You know, Matthew, this is really a dumb thing to be doing at 4:10 in the morning," she said to her son. "Somebody could come by and hit your dad on the head and take all our money out of our account."

At that moment a shadowy form materialized out of the darkness and stepped to the door of the little bank, watching Tom. Life went into slow motion for Gail. She saw Tom turn and walk toward the stranger, reaching out his hand to open the door.

No! she screamed silently. *Don't do it!*

But he did, and the door of the bank closed behind him. The two of them stood facing each other, Tom with his cash clutched in his hand and the other person grasping three large lumpy bags.

152

They began to talk as they moved toward the car. The stranger, bulky in many layers of clothing and wearing gloves and a knit hat pulled low over the face, defied gender identification.

Gail didn't know whether to bolt from the car and run for help or fly to her husband's defense. (Standing at less than five feet, she probably wouldn't have done more than scratch a couple kneecaps.) In the end, she remained paralyzed in a corner of the back seat.

Tom leaned down and tapped on the window, motioning for her to roll down the window. "This person needs a ride to the bus stop down the road. Do you think it's a good idea?"

Are you kidding? Gail wanted to shout. Instead, she tried to key into that special mental telepathy that husbands and wives sometimes use to figure out what he really wanted her to say, but it was so dark she couldn't see his face clearly.

Her prayer of less than an hour ago flashed across her mind. *I know I said that, Lord,* she argued silently, *but I don't think this is really something I want to do. It's definitely not the kind of experience I had in mind when I asked You to send someone across our path.* Then she heard herself saying out loud, "I guess it would be all right."

The stranger crowded into the other half of the back seat, letting go of the bags only long enough to pull off the knit cap, releasing a tumble of long hair.

So, she's a woman, Gail thought, not sure whether she was relieved or not.

"This is really kind of you and your family to do this for me," the woman said. She must have seen the fright in Gail's eyes because she added, "I won't harm you in any way. You can trust me. I am a Christian. Before I left this morning I asked the Lord to send Christian people to help me get where I need to go."

The air was electric. "We are Christians, too," Gail said. Her eyes met Tom's in the rearview mirror. She eyed their new passenger. "Doesn't it scare you, being out in the middle of the night like this? Where are you going, anyway?"

"No, I'm not frightened because I prayed to God for protec-

> **The stranger, bulky in many layers of clothing and wearing gloves and a knit hat pulled low over the face, defied gender identification.**

tion. I plan to catch the bus to Washington, D.C., then buy a ticket for as far as my money will take me and thumb it the rest of the way." She looked around at the loaded car. "It looks like you folks are traveling. Where are you going?"

Without giving it a second thought, Tom responded, "We're on our way to Florida."

"Really! That's where *I'm* going!" the woman exclaimed. "Do you think it would be possible for me to ride along with you?"

Tom stopped the car on the shoulder of the road. A great silence filled the car. It was one thing to take somebody a mile down the road to the bus stop, but quite another to consider spending 18 hours in the same car with a stranger. "Why are you going to Florida? Do you have family there?" he asked finally, buying time to think.

If the woman noticed his alarm, she didn't let on. She said her 94-year-old grandmother, her only living relative, was dying, and she had to get to Florida to see her. Again she asked, "Since you're going that way, would you mind very much if I rode along with you? I'll be no burden at all in any way. I'll just sit back here on my side of the car and not even talk, if you don't want me to."

After another silent rearview mirror conference Gail heard herself say, "That will be no problem. We'll just take it a step at a time and see how things go." She couldn't believe her own voice!

"Well, if you prayed, who am I to say no," Tom said quietly. "Let's pray again before we get on the road."

He pulled onto the interstate and headed south. "We'll be going as far as Macon, Georgia, today. I have some business there," Tom told her. "Once we get there, we'll decide what to do next."

"Since we're going to be together for a while we should introduce ourselves. I'm Mary." She extended a hand toward Gail.

Gail introduced herself and her family, then said, "It's nice you are a Christian. What religion are you?"

Mary laughed. "Well, I've tried the Baptists, Methodists,

Catholics, and the Pentecostals. I guess you would call me interdenominational. What are you?"

"We're Seventh-day Adventists. Have you ever heard of them?" Gail asked.

Mary's eyes got big. "Oh, yes! I know several things about Seventh-day Adventists. One thing is they really help people who are in need. And they go to church on Saturday. But the thing that really fascinates me is that they include footwashing with the Communion service. That's what Christ did when He was on this earth, you know." Her voice softened. "I would love to experience that."

At mid-morning the family stopped for breakfast, inviting Mary to join them. She declined politely, reminding them of her promise at the beginning of the trip to not be a burden. But she did agree to keep them company in the restaurant.

They made quite an entrance—Tom, Matthew, and Gail, followed by Mary, toting all her bags. Everything she had in the world must have been in those bags because she refused to leave them in the car. People stared at them. It was a little embarrassing. While the family ate their breakfast, Mary had a pear and a slice of cheese that she produced from one of her bags. She asked the waitress for a cup of hot water—if there was no charge.

Once back in the car, she laid her head back and closed her eyes. "I hope you don't mind," she apologized. "I haven't slept for a long time."

While she slept, Gail stole glances at her. From résumés and letters of referral she had shown them, she was obviously intelligent and well-educated and had held several important jobs, one with a New York publishing firm Tom was familiar with. As she began to unlayer in the warmth of the car it was apparent that her clothes were of high quality, some of them with designer labels.

And it was also apparent that she was wearing everything she owned—big overcoat, sports jacket, sweater, blouse, slacks, and wool scarf. Everything about her—her well-kept hair, designer glasses, even lipstick and nail polish—belied the bag-lady image.

As the miles rolled by, the Kapustas learned small pieces of her

> While she slept, Gail stole glances at her. Everything about her belied the bag-lady image.

155

history, but she was always careful to not give anything too specific. Her father and mother were married for a short time, then decided to divorce, giving their 3-month-old daughter to the grandmother and disappearing from her life forever. She never saw them again and said she didn't really care to. It was a part of her life she didn't want to talk about.

She had been married once, but the marriage didn't turn out well. She didn't want to talk about that, either. She had suffered a shoulder injury that required surgery and rehabilitation. Somehow, she had lost her job and had been out of work ever since.

Learning that all three Kapustas worked in a publishing house, she became almost animated, expressing a great interest in their work. She was very knowledgeable about presses and the publishing process and said she'd like to visit the Review and Herald Publishing Association sometime.

When they neared the place where their paths would divide, Tom pulled to the side of the road and turned to her. "Can we take you to the bus station or train depot and get you a ticket for Florida?" he asked.

"No, no," she assured him, "just let me make a phone call." She rummaged in her bags and pulled out a small directory. When she crossed the street to use the phone, she left her bags behind. For some reason, Gail felt good about that. Returning to the car, she handed Tom a piece of paper on which she'd written directions to an address just outside Macon, Georgia. "I have friends there," she said shortly.

When they were almost to Macon, Gail turned to her and said, "I would like to give you Tom's business card. I've written our home address and phone number on the back. When you come back to Hagerstown, make sure you call us and we'll give you a tour of the publishing house. We'll eat in the cafeteria and share a little bit of our work with you. But you know what I'd really like?"

Mary smiled at her new friend's enthusiasm. "No, but I think you're going to tell me!"

"I'd like you to come to our house some Friday afternoon and

156

we'll get ready for the Sabbath and have sundown worship together. We'll get up in the morning and go to church, then come home and have Sabbath dinner and spend this special time with the Lord and each other before closing the Sabbath with family worship."

The woman promised she'd call.

By this time they had driven down a small lane and stopped in front of a wide aluminum gate festooned with Christmas wreaths. A collie, tail wagging furiously in welcome, watched them with friendly interest from behind the gate. Beyond, a ranch-style house stood at the far end of the lane.

Mary gathered her bags together and put her hat back on, becoming once again the person they had picked up at dawn. "Thank you so much for the ride . . . and for our new friendship."

Suddenly, Gail didn't want her to go, couldn't let her go. "Now remember the promise we have between us."

"I'll remember," Mary smiled.

"In order for us to keep our promise you will have to call me, because I have no way to get in contact with you."

The two women hugged and kissed each other on the cheek. Gail looked directly into her eyes. "I'll be praying for you, Mary. And when you come back, I want to wash your feet at Communion."

Tears flooded the woman's eyes.

"I want to give you some money for your trip. Would you be offended?"

Mary lifted her chin. "Yes, I would. Our Lord will take care of me." She got quickly out of the car. Slipping through the gate, she walked down the lane, turning briefly to wave, then was gone.

Tom looked at his wife. "Are you going to cry?"

"I think so." Her backseat companion was gone. She was going to miss her. *Lord, please protect her wherever she is going . . . we really help people who are in need . . . we go to church on Saturday . . . we include footwashing in the Communion service . . . And one more thing, Mary—in ministering we are always ministered to.*

Mary gathered her bags together and put her hat back on, becoming once again the person they had picked up at dawn.

157

That's Not All, Folks!

There's not enough room in this book for all the stories we came across about ordinary people doing extraordinary things—painting the world with love. For that matter, as you read perhaps a story came to *your* mind that would benefit someone else if they heard about it. If so, would you please jot down the particulars (you don't have to write it all out) and send it to Book Editor, Review and Herald Publishing Association, 55 West Oak Ridge Drive, Hagerstown, MD 21740. Include your name and address and phone number (don't forget the area code). Perhaps your story will be included in the next book!

More exciting stories about Adventists making a difference

Gifted Hands, by Ben Carson, M.D., with Cecil Murphey. Looking at the big zero on his test paper, he thought he was the dumbest kid in school. But this ghetto youth left his failing grades and murderous temper behind to become director of pediatric neurosurgery at Johns Hopkins Hospital. Medical breakthroughs—such as the critical separation of the Binder twins in 1987—have brought this Adventist worldwide acclaim. But as the media flock to him for interviews, he gives God the glory. Dr. Carson's autobiography reassures us of God's constant leading and His strong personal interest in our lives. Hardcover, 232 pages. US$12.95, Cdn$16.20.

Katrina Stands Alone, by Natelkka E. Burrell. Separated from her parents, abused and despised by her grandmother, Katrina rose above her past to become a distinguished teacher, honoring her Lord and receiving honor for her contribution to her students. Paperback, 95 pages. US$6.95, Cdn$8.70.

Plane Crash, by Michael Diamond. The Cessna 150 plunged toward the canyon wall. The pilot grabbed the controls, but it was too late. When he regained consciousness, his troubles had only begun! A thrilling drama of one man's remarkable endurance and indestructible faith. Paperback, 95 pages. US$6.95, Cdn$8.70.

Promise Deferred, by Siegfried H. Horn. Interned in a POW camp the author found a Bible promise: God sets the prisoners free. But Horn remained a POW, facing starvation and mind-wrecking boredom. However, as God paused in fulfilling His promise, He was preparing this missionary for a new career. Paperback, 95 pages. US$7.50, Cdn$9.40.

Faith Under Fire, by Wellesley Muir. Open this book and you'll find yourself swept up into action, danger, faith, suspense, miracles, and God's redeeming love. It's the story of Leo Pinedo, who was drafted into the Peruvian army and opposed by a cruel captain determined to crush his convictions. Paperback, 122 pages. US$7.95, Cdn$9.95.

Mac & Wife, by Eleanor Jackson. A first-person story about faith in the rough-and-ready days of the rural West. The author and her new minister-husband teamed up to bring God's word to gamblers, bootleggers, proud farmers, and hardened newspapermen in rural Idaho. Paper, 96 pages. US$6.95, Cdn$8.70.
